LEGENDS OF **DELAWARE** AUTO RACING

LEGENDS OF DELAWARE AUTO RACING

Chad Wayne Culver

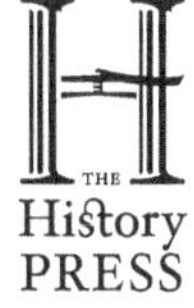

Published by The History Press
Charleston, SC
www.historypress.com

Front cover, top: courtesy of Don and Linda Allen, D&L Photos; *middle, left*: courtesy of Don and Linda Allen, D&L Photos; *middle, right*: courtesy of Don and Linda Allen, D&L Photos; *bottom*: courtesy of Snookie Vent.
Back cover, top: courtesy of Robert Wheatman; *top inset*: courtesy of David Grey; *bottom inset*: courtesy of Ken Covey.

First published 2019

Manufactured in the United States

ISBN 9781467138291

Library of Congress Control Number: 2019950035

In memoriam
Walt Breeding
1946–2018
My first racing hero.

CONTENTS

ACKNOWLEDGEMENTS

It has truly been an honor to write this book about so many of Delaware's dirt track heroes. I have thoroughly treasured my time interacting and speaking with everyone who was involved in this book. The completion of *Legends of Delaware Auto Racing* would not have been possible without the following people.

First and foremost, thank you to my wife, April, and daughter, Ava. Both are my number one supporters, and I could not do this without them. They both are my greatest inspirations. Thanks to my mom and dad, Wayne and Toni Culver, for their support as well. They are always willing to pick up photos or information or pick up some car parts for me, and their help and support are greatly appreciated. Many thanks to Don and Linda Allen of D&L Photos for helping supply a vast amount of the images in this book, and to early dirt track historian Phil Davis for helping to check the accuracy of the information about those early years of racing.

There are so many people who contributed to this book in big and small ways. Thank you to the following: Joe Ann Adams, Melvin Joseph Jr., P.J. Walker, Johnny Martin Jr., Haines Tull, Mike Lambert, Becky Reed, Michael Reed, Bill Lawson, Kirk Lawson, the Pettyjohn family, Bobby Sapp, the White family, David Hill, Walt Breeding and family, Charlie Cathell, Charlie Brown, Snookie Vent, Billy Towers, the Dutton family, Eugene Mills, Paul Mills, Ken Covey, Ron Slade, Bill Garn, Richard Childress, Jimmy Messick, Irene Rust, Lou Johnson, Richard Jarvis Jr., Harold Bunting, Hal Browning, Bobby Wilkins, Gary Trice, David Trice, Brad Trice, Bob and Debbie

Geiger, Ron Keys, Earl Keys, Charlie Brown, Curt Michael, Ricky Elliot, Brett Deyo, Rick Sweeten Images, Landstone Photography, Louis O'Neal, Burt Quillin, Cy Clendaniel, Betty Wyatt-Dix and Tom Jerman.

Most important, thank you to the many fans of racing who have offered words of encouragement and great conversation during the completion of this book. You are the backbone of racing, and your enthusiasm is contagious. I'll see you at the track!

INTRODUCTION

legend | 'lejənd

1. A traditional story sometimes popularly regarded as historical but unauthenticated.
2. An extremely famous or notorious person, especially in a particular field.

Almost immediately after the completion of my first book, *Delaware Auto Racing*, I wanted to dig deeper into the lives of some of Delaware's best-known, most-beloved, longest-running and most successful characters involved in auto racing. I wanted to tell the stories of the First State's legends of auto racing. Delaware has had its fair share of characters who are extremely well known in the racing community, both here in Delaware and throughout the country. The contributions these individuals made to racing in Delaware, whether it be as a driver, car owner, track promoter, builder or supporter of racing have been significant and have elevated racing in the First State to what it is today. From the perfectly groomed dirt tracks of Delaware International Speedway and Georgetown Speedway to the high banks of NASCAR's Dover International Speedway, this book tells the story of each legend and the sacrifices, glory, heartache and reward each has experienced during their time in this sport.

Despite Delaware's small size, the history and heritage of racing in the state rivals that of any in America. The stories told in the following pages represent normal, blue-collar, hardworking, everyday people who do extraordinary things in racing and in life and have left a lasting legacy of greatness in Delaware's racing community. My hope is that these stories help bring light to the background of these local racing heroes and the contributions made by not only those listed in this book but also by all of those involved in racing in Delaware. With that being said, the pages of this book are simply not big enough to house all of those who have made contributions to racing in Delaware throughout the years. The names listed and chosen for this book are simply part of what I hope to be the first volume of more books on those who have made an impact on racing in Delaware. The names in the book are not in any particular order and were not chosen based on popularity but on their contribution to racing in their given area.

Racing roots run deep in Delaware, and many of the families involved in the sport now have their third or even fourth generation involved in some aspect of racing. You could find family names like Hill, Pettyjohn, White, Wilkins, Mills, Dutton, Trice, Vent and Bunting on various track programs from the 1950s, '60s, '70s and '80s, yet today, if you visit the track, you will find new generations of racers with those last same names carrying on the family tradition. Great contributions do not stop with the drivers; many people behind the scenes make racing a success. Car builders, owners and sponsors like Norris "Speedy" Reed, Walt Messick, Eugene and Paul Mills, Walt Breeding, Ken Covey and many others all play an important part in racing's success in the area. Also not to be left out are the track owners and promoters. The Cathell family has owned Delaware International Speedway and promoted races there for well over half of a century. Brett Deyo has recently breathed new life into Georgetown Speedway, which was started in 1949 by Melvin Joseph. All have left an indelible mark on auto racing that has cast a wide net of influence in Delaware and in other racing communities across the nation. Indeed, racing in Delaware has had a historic, influential past and looks to be leading the way to an exciting future.

1

MELVIN JOSEPH

1921-2005

To find a prime example of excellence, determination, performance and passion in not only motorsports but also in life, you need look no further than the life of Melvin Joseph. The son of Harry and Ella Mae Joseph, Melvin Joseph was born in Georgetown, Delaware, on August 4, 1921. From a young age, Melvin showed the vision and determination necessary to be successful in business and life. The well-told story of a sixth-grade Joseph leaving school to join the circus as an equipment mechanic, only to return and take a $300 loan from his grandmother and turn it into the Melvin L. Joseph Construction Company, is a lesson that includes all the values that would guide him throughout his life.

The year 1949 would be a life-altering one for Melvin Joseph. In '49, Joseph secured his first major state contract, became a partner in a local Ford dealership and constructed the half-mile dirt racetrack that would be known as Georgetown Speedway. Joseph declared 49 his lucky number, and for the rest of his life, his license plates, horses, planes and race cars all contained that number. Joseph approached racing with the same passion and determination that made him a successful businessman. His first driver, Johnny Stoltzfus, recalled in a 2014 interview what it was like to drive for him. "He was the definition of what a great car owner should be. The cars were always meticulously prepared and set up, but above all else Melvin was concerned about safety. That was a time when safety was often thought about last, but Melvin cared about people and always made sure the cars were safe. I think that said a lot about him."

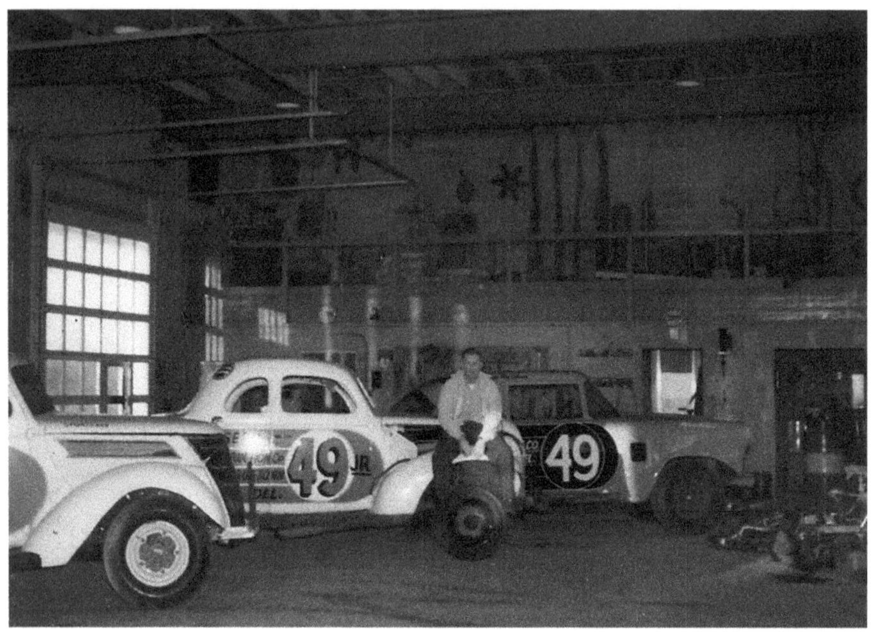

Melvin Joseph relaxing by three of his early race cars. *Courtesy of the Melvin Joseph family.*

Stoltzfus was the first in a long line of drivers who would drive for Joseph. Other notable drivers who piloted cars were Dean Pelton, George Hudick, Johnny Martin, Johnny Roberts, Dick Kaufman, Ken Marriott, George Harrison, Gene Loveless, Reds Kagle, Vince Conrad, Larry Frank, Melvin Joseph Jr., Fonty Flock, Banjo Matthews, Ralph Moody, Tiny Lund, Curtis Turner, Joe Weatherly, Marvin Panch, David Pearson and Bobby Allison. Joseph's cars won not only on the local dirt tracks but also at the top levels of the sport in NASCAR competition. Whether it was Banjo Matthews and Vince Conrad winning both the Sportsman and Modified race on the beach at Daytona in 1955 in Joseph's cars, or Bobby Allison's win in NASCAR Grand National competition at Bowman Grey Stadium, no. 49 was a force to be reckoned with.

When interest was shown about building a NASCAR superspeedway in Delaware, it was Joseph who led the charge. He paved the way with his established relationships in NASCAR to build Dover International Speedway, which held its first race in 1969. Melvin L. Joseph Construction was contracted to build the one-mile oval speedway, which holds a five-eighths-mile horse track inside of it. Joseph held the position of director of auto racing at the speedway until his passing in 2005. He also gave the command for drivers to start their engines at every race from 1969 to 2005. Always looking forward and thinking of ways to improve things, Joseph was also an innovator in racing. He was the first to use a solid boilerplate wall on a speedway to improve safety and cut cost. He also was required to come up with unique construction techniques when building and repaving Dover International Speedway. Between the 1994 and 1995 racing seasons, the track was repaved and changed from asphalt to concrete, a task some said could not be done on the steep banks of twenty-four degrees. Once again, Joseph was up to the task, partnering with John and Tom Madden of Atlantic Contracting. They designed specialty equipment to span the entire track and make a seamless concrete racing surface.

Melvin Joseph's legacy can be seen all over the Delmarva Peninsula, from Georgetown Speedway to Dover International Speedway. The stories told from unknown numbers of racers of how he would help them behind the scenes just to make the next race all point to a man who loved auto racing and loved the people involved in it. Without his contributions to racing in Delaware, the sport would look much different than it does today. One could

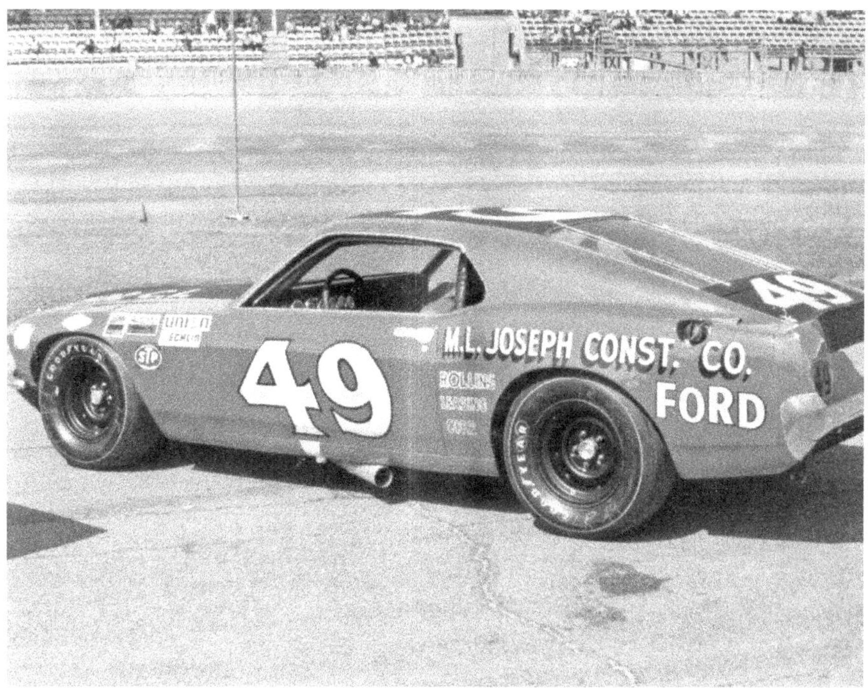

The no. 49 Grand American Mustang owned by Melvin Joseph and driven by NASCAR Hall of Famers Bobby Allison and David Pearson. *Courtesy of the Melvin Joseph family.*

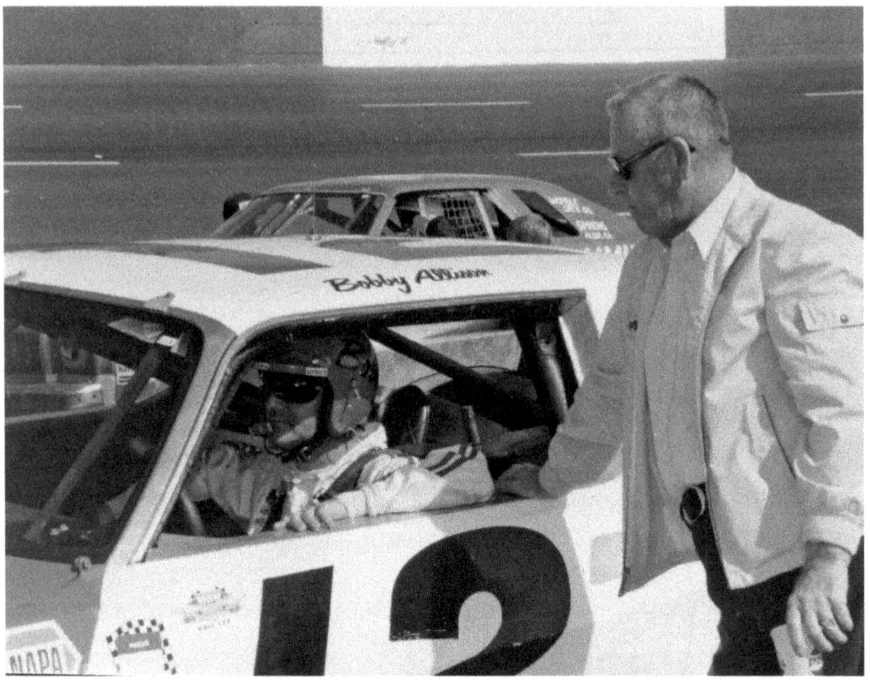

Melvin Joseph and his friend Bobby Allison have a last-minute word before Allison hits the track. *Courtesy of the Melvin Joseph family.*

certainly call Melvin Joseph "The Father of Auto Racing in Delaware" for all of his dedication to the sport.

On March 17, 2018, just one day shy of the sixty-eighth anniversary of the first race at Joseph's beloved Georgetown Speedway, thousands of race fans, local politicians and members of the Joseph family gathered to honor Joseph and the track he built at the annual Melvin L. Joseph Memorial Race by unveiling a State of Delaware Historic Marker. The marker was inscribed:

> *"Georgetown Speedway."*
> *Built in 1949 by businessman and auto racing pioneer Melvin L. Joseph, many racing legends got their start at Georgetown's half-mile dirt oval. The Delaware Stock Car Racing Association sanctioned the first race at the speedway on March 18, 1950. The speedway was NASCAR sanctioned from 1953 to 1957 and from 1959 to 1963. Over the years, the Georgetown Speedway has become well known across the country for its role in the development of stock-car racing.*

2
PAUL WALKER
1930–1988

Long before the actor Paul Walker became famous in the popular *Fast and Furious* series of movies, another popular Paul Walker was tearing up the dirt tracks of the East Coast, securing his place as a legend of Delaware auto racing. Originally from Shakerstown, Pennsylvania, Walker's father worked for Bethlehem Steel and would visit and stay in one of the many beach cottages located in Lewes, Delaware, to vacation and rest from the hard work at the steel plant. Falling in love with Delaware, the young Walker decided to make his home in Sussex County, get married and settle down. It would not be long before the eighteen-year-old would find his way behind the wheel of a stock car. His son Paul Walker Jr. explains how the family found out about his racing and how his dad got started during the early years of racing on the shore.

> *Dad got started driving the no. 2P car for Ernie Lynch. He lived in the same area of Lewes as my Mom and Dad did. My mom did not even know he was driving a race car for almost a year. That was in 1948 and my dad was only eighteen years old. Dad was going to the races with his brother Bill and was helping him with his race car, but then someone told my mom, "Ma'am, your husband is a hell of a stock car driver!" She told them, "You must mean my husband's brother, Bill." They told my mom, "No! It was Paul, we saw him running down at Love Creek." So he was busted, and that's how we found out about his racing. He was running at Love Creek and Nanticoke and some of the early speedways. Tracks were popping up everywhere, as it was really the start of stock car racing during that time.*

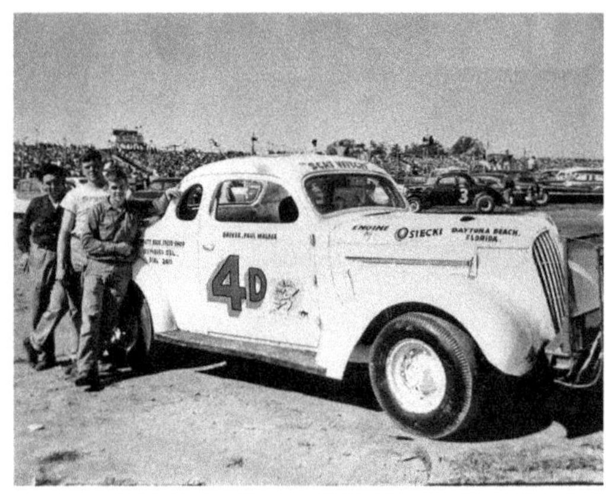

From left to right are Preston Niblett, Jerry Jenkins and Paul Walker standing next to the "Scat Witch" at the famous Langhorne Speedway. *Courtesy of Paul Walker Jr.*

During those pioneer days of racing, top drivers were in high demand. These brave young men piloted Modified and Sportsman cars to their absolute limit, often on tracks carved out of open fields with little regard to safety. Walker's skills caught the eye of the area's top owners, and the list of cars that Walker drove was indeed impressive. After cutting his teeth in the no. 2P of Ernie Lynch, he then drove the no. 21 Moore's Chevrolet car in the 1950–51 race season. During the 1953 season, Walker drove for several of the area's top owners, including the no. 49 of Melvin Joseph and the no. 71 of Wilson Todd. Walker ended the 1953 season driving the no. 4D of the Niblett Brothers and would drive for them until the end of 1956. Walker and the Niblett Brothers had great success with each other not only in Delaware, but outside the state as well. Walker won the first race ever at New Jersey's Vineland Speedway, winning the track's first heat race. He would go on to finish second to one of the East Coast's best and most popular drivers, Al Tasnady, in the feature event. Not one to settle for a second-place finish, Walker returned the following week to finish first in the feature against the East Coast's most skilled drivers. The year 1955 was huge for Walker at Georgetown Speedway as well. He won nine races in a season that had many rainouts and finished first in points at the speedway, beating out Horace Williams of Bridgeville, Delaware, for the track's NASCAR Sportsman Championship. Walker was also listed twelfth in NASCAR's National Sportsman points. Not bad for a team that raced close to home and rarely raced outside its home state. In the 1950s and early 1960s, records show that Walker had over forty feature wins at Georgetown Speedway alone. After leaving the Niblett Brothers at the end of 1956, Walker drove for the Ritter Brothers in the no. 11 and no. 12 cars for

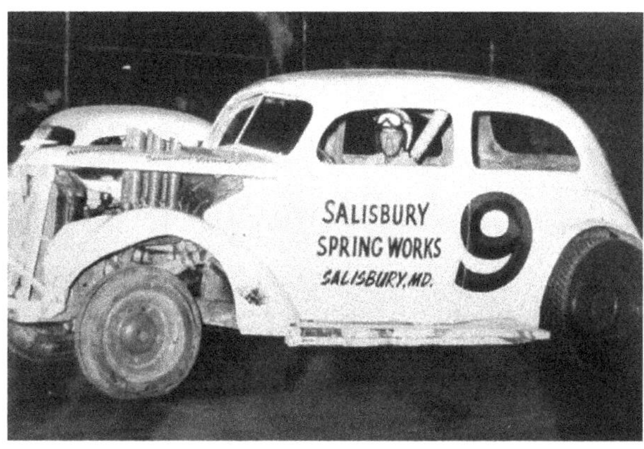

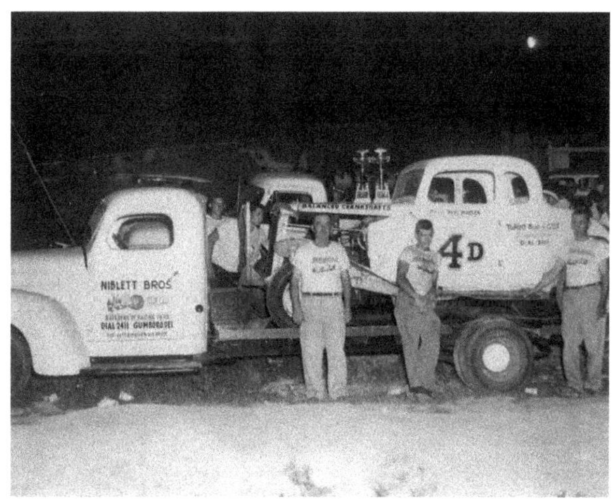

Top: Paul Walker behind the wheel of the "Mr. Frankie" Salisbury Spring Works no. 9 car built with the help of Frankie Schneider. *Courtesy of Paul Walker Jr.*

Right: Paul Walkers and car owners the Niblett Brothers relax next to their car hauler after a successful night of racing. *Courtesy of the Walker family*.

the 1957 season and the first part of 1958 before returning to the Wilson Todd no. 71 for the rest of 1958 and 1959.

The 1960 through 1964 seasons would find Walker in the Salisbury Spring Works no. 9 Modified, one of the area's top cars, built with the help of Frankie Schneider, who some consider to be the best Modified stock car driver ever. Schneider and Walker had done battle on the track many times in the past and would remain lifelong friends until Walker's passing in 1988. In a 2016 interview, the late Frankie Schneider talked about building that race car, racing in the 1950s and his old friend Paul Walker.

> *Paul was a good person and a good racer. You could trust him on the track. He was smooth and didn't do any funny stuff. A lot of those guys were all over the place, not Paul. I was asked to come down and help build the*

> *Salisbury Spring Works no. 9. It only took me a couple of days to cut one up and make it into a race car. I remember that area well. One time on Route 50, I found an old race car and brought it home. It had a fifty on the side of it because it was on Route 50 in Maryland. That car would later become my favorite race car, "Old Bess." Those were the best of times. It never got better than those days.*

Walker finished out his career driving the no. 6617 car for Bobby Parker in 1966 at Delmar Speedway and his own no. 4 car from 1967 to 1969 before handing the reins over to his sons, Paul Walker Jr. and Tom Walker. Drivers like Paul Walker were pioneers during racing's infancy in Delaware. Their heroics on the track and relationship with the fans set the standard for all others to follow. Paul Walker's success on the track and contributions to the sport not only make him a legend of Delaware auto racing but also a pioneer in the sport of auto racing as well.

3

JOHNNY MARTIN

1927–1992

The name Johnny Martin will always remain synonymous with stock car racing in southern Delaware. One of the first racers to truly become a local hero, Martin won the very first race at the historic Georgetown Speedway on March 18, 1950. For many people, it was their first time seeing a stock car race of any kind, and the bravery and skill Martin showed on the new speedway left a lasting impression that is talked about to this day. Martin got his start in racing in the spring of 1949, when he was taking a cruise in the family's Mercury and decided he would check out the stock car race happening in Magnolia, Delaware. Early newspaper reports show that after no more than fifteen minutes at the track, Martin decided he would enter the Mercury in the day's races. Surprising many, he went on to win his first race, an eight-lap heat race, and he finished third in the twenty-lap feature that same day. The car came out without a scratch, but when he returned the next week, he earned two dented fenders, so he decided to buy a stock car and save the family Mercury for the road. Martin bought his first stock car in partnership with Russell Hudson of Lewes, Delaware. The car was dubbed the "Orange Blossom Special." The team of Martin as driver and Hudson as the mechanic went on to win every race it entered at Magnolia Speedway. During his career, Martin would pilot many of the top rides in Delaware, including the Orange Blossom Special of Russell Hudson, the Mitchell's Hatchery no. 5, the no. 1 of George Bowers, the no. 49 owned by Melvin Joseph, the no. 191 of Dutch Warrington, the no. 39 of Francis Prettyman, the no. 97 of Doug Morgan, the no. 3D of Howard Davis and the no. 231 of Ed Henry.

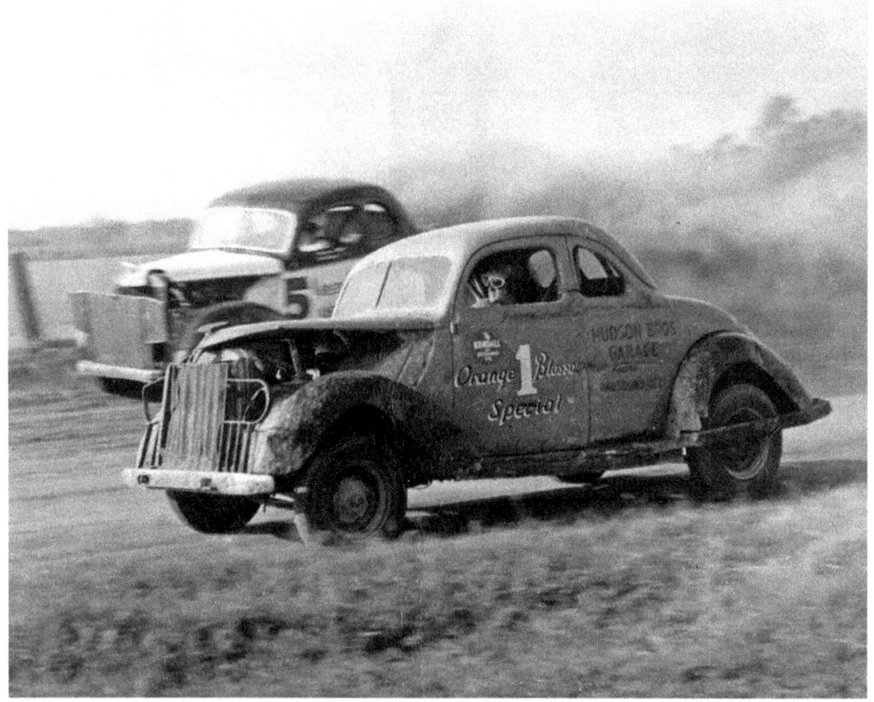

Johnny Martin thunders through the corner in his no. 1 Orange Blossom Special. *Courtesy of Horace Williams Jr.*

Martin was a fan favorite and won the most popular driver award several times at Georgetown Speedway. It is often said that racers are ordinary people who do extraordinary things. Local fans of racing at the time must have seen this quality in Johnny Martin. Here was one of their own who lived in the area and was just like them out on the track, winning races and championships. Johnny Martin Jr. gives us some insight about his father's humble beginnings and sheds some light on why he may have been one of the most likeable and popular drivers of the time.

> *Dad started out being a farmer and really did not like that too much. Then, he became a cop in Lewes, Delaware. I remember the local paper doing an article on the flying cop of Lewes because of his racing. Then, he ended up being a captain at the prison over in Georgetown. He would often work nighttime a lot, but on race night, he would work until 8:00 p.m. and then have someone come in and relieve him so he could come over to the track. He would come over and race and would never have time*

> *to warm the car up. He would just get straight into it and go race. Dad was always a clean driver. I think the fans liked that and he had a lot of fans. He never was much for partying like some of the other teams at the tracks. When I was a kid, I always used to get so excited after the races were over because he would take me into town to get a soda and celebrate if he did well that night.*

Although car owners, track owners and drivers tried their best to keep racing as safe as possible, the sport was still in its infancy on the shore, and safety measures were still sometimes crude. Look at any car today that raced in the 1950s and you will be amazed at the bravery of the drivers and wonder how more were not seriously injured. Unfortunately, it would be an accident that would cause Johnny Martin's career to come to a stop while he was driving the no. 231 for Ed Henry. It was a career-ending wreck that he was lucky to survive, as his son remembers well.

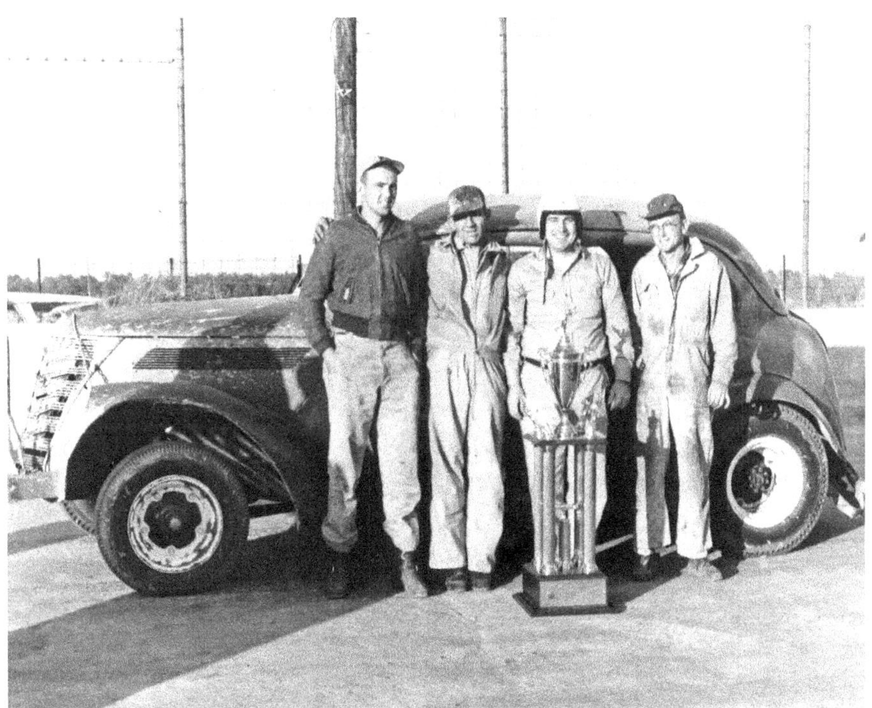

Posing with the no. 231 from left to right are Alfred "Tacky" Reddish, Ed Henry, Johnny Martin and Robert "Wheaty" Wheatman. *Courtesy of Robert Wheatman.*

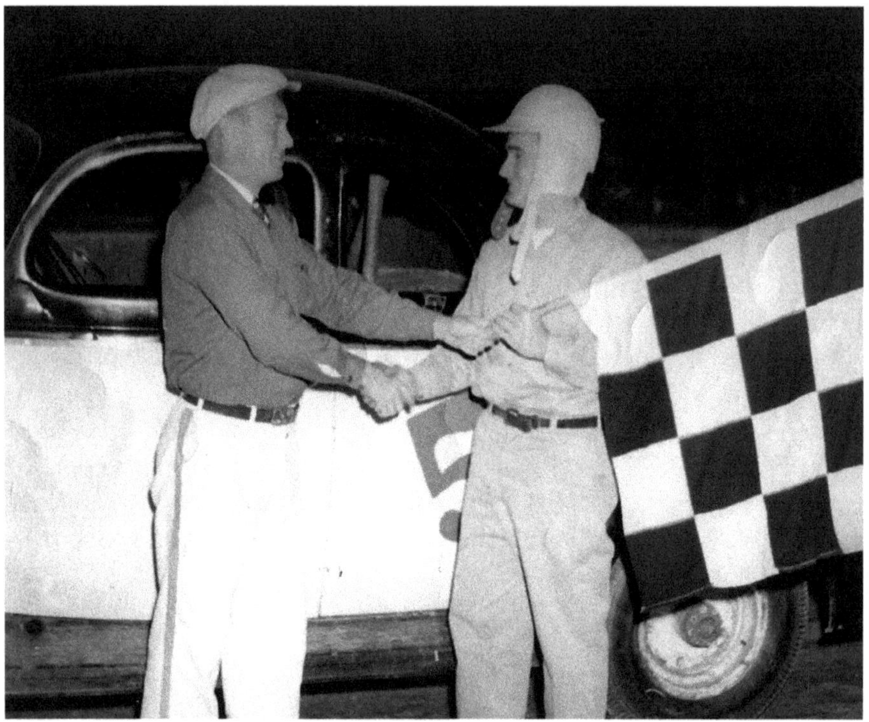

Flagman Ton Brown (*left*) presents the checkered flag to driver Johnny Martin for winning another feature event. *Courtesy of Charlie Brown.*

> *Dad had three or four bad wrecks during his career. I remember one wreck early on in the no. 3D for car owner Howard Davis. He came home all black and blue. Back then, Georgetown had a steep bank, and if you went off it the right way, you were in for a heck of a ride. A couple of his worst wrecks were when he was driving for Ed Henry and of course that last one was really bad. We had a newer body sitting on a 1937 Ford frame and the wheels stuck out from the body somewhat. He hopped over another car's wheel going into turn three and the car just barrel-rolled off the third turn. It crushed the top of the car in. That one was real serious and it took him a long time to recover from that and that was the last race he ever ran.*

Looking back at these early pioneers of racing, one has to appreciate the bravery and spirit they had. Drivers like Johnny Martin and others from that era set the standard and laid the foundation for racing in Delaware. Their approachability and actions on and off the track made them everyday heroes, entertaining thousands of people every week when racing reigned supreme. Fans would travel to the tracks to see one of their own doing extraordinary things and forget about the problems of life, if just for a few hours. Drivers like Johnny Martin live on; their spirit can be seen to this day every week at the tracks, where you will see a new generation of drivers living up to the standards that these pioneers set so long ago.

4
HAINES TULL

Sometimes, being in the right place at the right time pays off in racing. Such was the case for Haines Tull. Tull started his racing career like most up-and-coming racers, in go-karts. During his early years of involvement in racing, Tull enjoyed racing karts alongside his daughters. One day, he was approached by legendary car owner Howard Davis to drive for him.

Davis had owned race cars for a while. I had watched his cars for many years at Georgetown with J.R. Jones driving and Horace Williams. Walt Breeding was supposed to drive the car and for some reason that fell through and Davis came and just asked me, "Hey Haines! You want to drive a stock car for me?" When I said I didn't know nothing about them, Davis said, "Well there is not really a whole lot to know." So I took the job and really found out there was a lot to know about those cars. At the time, Walt Breeding and Ken Covey built about eight or nine rolling chassis Tobias kit cars, and the only thing I really did was go over to Walt's place and help put the body on the car.

Tull would end up racing five years for car owner Davis. In their second year as a team, they added a second car to the stable, driven by Walt Breeding. Tull fondly remembers his teammate:

I knew Walt well from Karting. He was ten years younger than me, and I remember his grandfather, who we used to call "Pop," taking him around

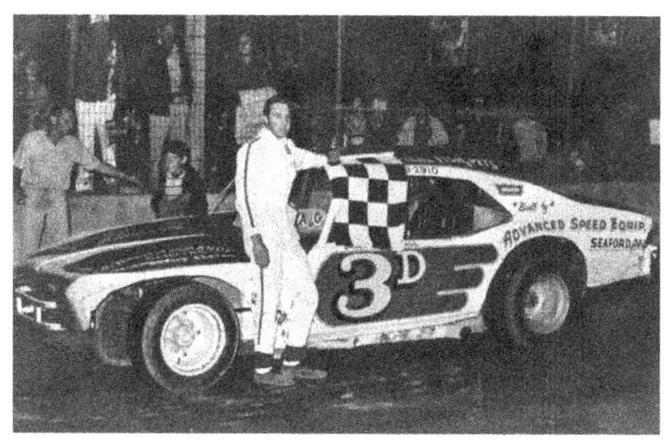

Driving one of the first Tobias chassis cars in the area, Haines Tull poses with the checkered flag after another victory. *Author's collection.*

> *to race. During our first year racing, Walt pretty much more or less worked on the cars, but did not drive. I think Speedy Reed and Walt Messick were involved in that second year because our cars were painted the same, but mine was no. 3D and Walt's was no. 1. He was constantly changing the suspension on the cars to try to make them better. He was a thinker and was always trying to make the cars better.*

Tull was famous for his consistency and ability to stay out of trouble, and he credits that for his incredible success during his career.

> *We never had the fastest car on the track, we tried to get the car to handle well and the engines used at the time only cost four thousand dollars. They were standard bore and standard stroke big blocks. Nothing fancy. When the cost of the engines started going to thirty thousand dollars, I said it was probably time for me to quit because I was into it for the fun of it. When Walt Breeding built me a car after I stopped driving for Howard Davis, it was eight thousand dollars for a rolling chassis. So, we had less than fifteen thousand dollars in the whole car. I always tried to finish in the top five. I knew I did not have the fastest car, but a lot of times the fastest car would break down and not make it to the finish. Some people ran so hard the tires would wear out or the equipment could not finish. Sometimes we just hit on things though, like one year we won six races in a row at Georgetown.*

Just a glance at the records reveals the consistency that made Tull famous. For seven consecutive years, Tull won a championship at either Georgetown Speedway or Delaware International Speedway; some years, he won both. When asked about his toughest competitors and the best racers he competed against, Tull comes up with a few names immediately.

> *Harold Bunting was as tough as they come. Never had no trouble with him. He was a clean driver. Just really good! One of my favorite wins was the first time I won at Harrington. I beat Harold by two feet. The worst one was my old friend Walt Breeding. He turned me over twice! One was at Harrington and we were teammates. We were just practicing! Howard Davis gave him heck over that one. I really ran good at Harrington Fair. No one could ever figure it out, but I only changed one thing on the car when I went from Georgetown Speedway to Harrington, and that was the right rear shock. I went one number lighter on it to give me more roll in the car. Eddie Pettyjohn was a good chauffer also. I remember when he won something like eleven races in a row over at Little Lincoln Speedway and there was some kind of deal or a bounty for anyone that could beat Pettyjohn at that track. We went over there and finished second the first week. We had never run there before and came home and changed a few things. We went back the next week and passed him on the outside to win the race.*

The race contested by two of the best in Delaware was a glimpse into the future of racing around the country. Racing was in a transition in the early 1970s, and this win was significant, as it symbolized a transition in equipment

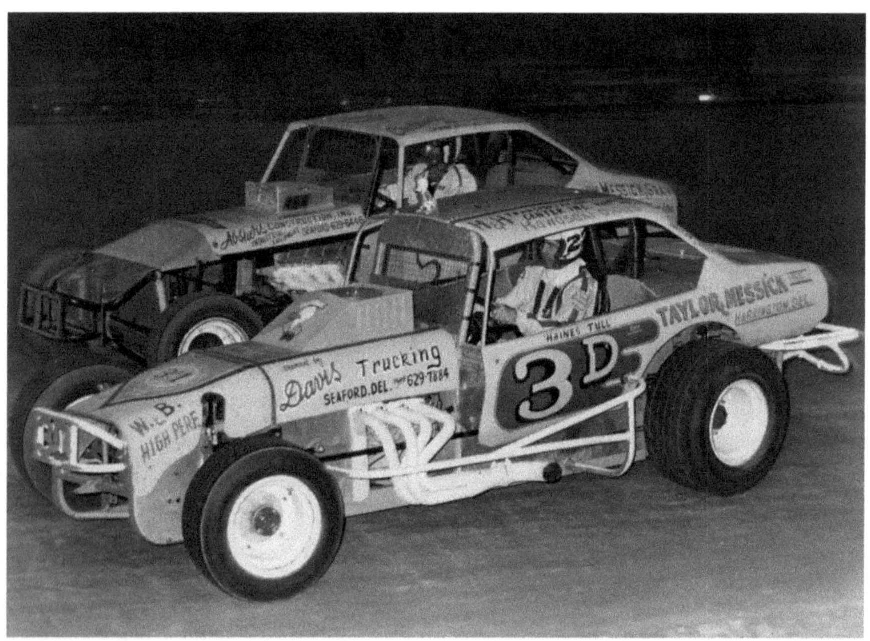

Haines Tull running the low groove in the Howard Davis no. 3. *Courtesy of David Grey.*

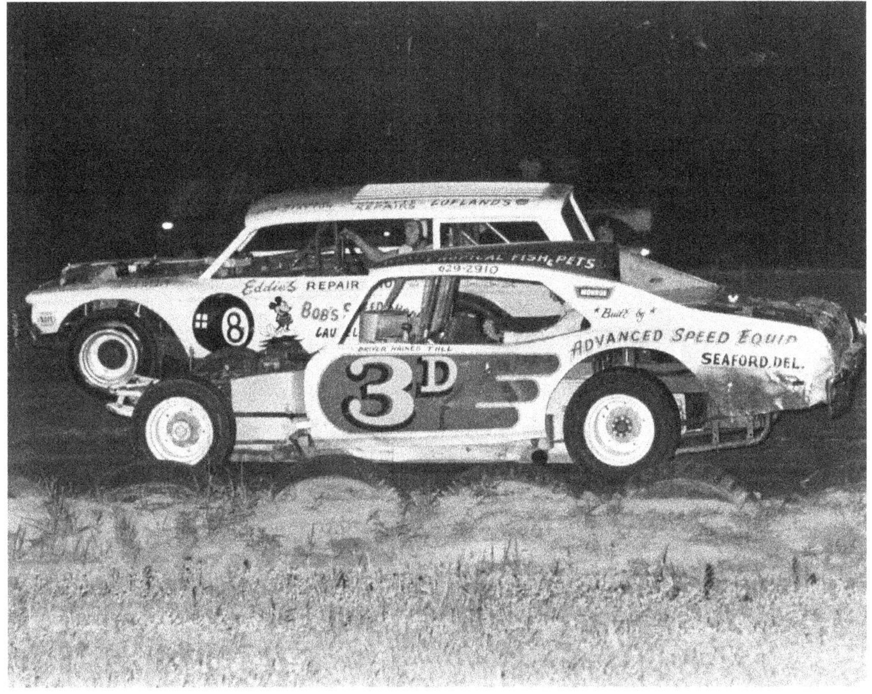

When Haines Tull drove his new Tobias chassis race car to victory at Little Lincoln Speedway, it signaled a change in race-car design. *Courtesy of David Grey.*

and performance. On the way out were the homemade chassis that drivers would find in junkyards around the Delmarva Peninsula. The writing on the wall was clear: race-specific chassis were the wave of the future and would forever change the direction of racing in Delaware.

In a relativity short and successful career that spanned from 1972 to 1979, Haines has no regrets about his time in racing. Racing and winning on every track in Delaware at the time, Tull's statistics are the envy of any racer. Today, the active Haines Tull lives west of Seaford, Delaware, and still enjoys going to the races every now and then, perhaps to reminisce about his days behind the wheel. He's a gentleman in every sense of the word. If you see him at the track, say "hi" and enjoy a conversation with a true racing legend.

5

NORRIS "SPEEDY" REED

1928–1995

The story of Norris "Speedy" Reed almost reads like a script for a movie. A farmer from Smithville, Maryland, a small rural area near Federalsburg, Maryland, near the Delaware border, wins the Daytona 500 pole. But this is no movie script; that is exactly what happened at the 1976 Daytona 500. An underdog car owned by Reed and piloted by driver Ramo Stott won the pole position at the biggest race of the year in what would be an upset for the ages. Daytona Speedway was a long way from the dirt tracks of southern Delaware, and Speedy's accomplishment encapsulated what it was to dream big and shoot for the stars. Long before those days of glory at Daytona, Speedy, as everyone called him, got his start driving on the dusty local tracks of Delaware, driving his own "no. 2 John Deere" car at tracks like Myers, Nanticoke and Georgetown Speedways under the Delaware Stock Car Racing Association. Not long after he started driving, he caught the attention of Ed Henry, an owner based in Denton, Maryland, and started to drive his no. 38 for several races. During the time when NASCAR became the sanctioning body at Georgetown Speedway, Speedy joined forces with Bill Cummings of Ridgley, Maryland, to form the no. 141 race team. The team's baby blue 1937 Ford Coach became a fixture in the Modified Sportsman events in the area. Even in those early days, Speedy ventured outside the area to race at some of the East Coast's top speedways. His nephew Mike Reed remembers traveling to the races as a child with his uncle.

I remember going to Reading Speedway in Pennsylvania with him as a child with the no. 141. He would tell us stories about going over to Beltsville Speedway which was over by Washington back when there was no Chesapeake Bay Bridge and there was only a ferry. He would say that after the race, they would bust their tail to get back to the ferry because it closed at twelve o'clock and if you missed it, you would have to sleep in the truck and come back in the morning when the ferry opened again.

During those early days of car ownership, a young Walt Breeding who lived close by started to help on Speedy's farm. It was not long before Breeding became part of the race team and began to hone his fabrication skills on Speedy's race cars. With an equal love of racing, the two would remain lifelong friends and partners and have much success in the Modified and Late Model divisions up and down the East Coast. The Taylor & Messick–sponsored no. 1 car owned by Speedy Reed and driven by Walt Breeding would form one of the most iconic teams to ever race in the First

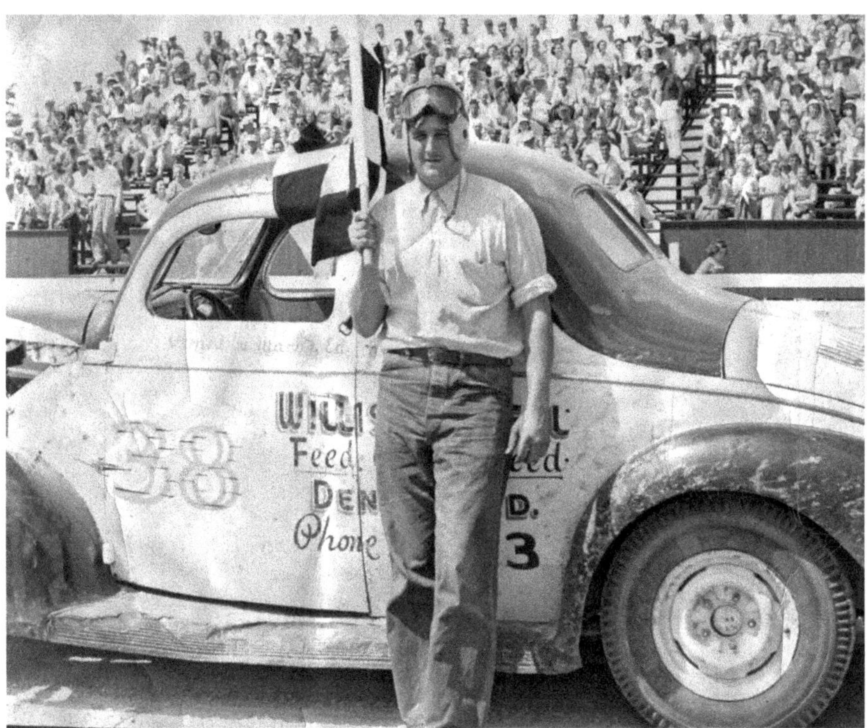

A young Norris "Speedy" Reed holds the checkered flag after a hard-fought victory in the Ed Henry–owned no. 38. *Photo by Malcom E. Lord, courtesy of Becky Reed.*

State. Perhaps the reason for so much success was the similar personalities of Speedy and his driver. Mike Reed remembers the innovative drive that both of them possessed.

> *They were both so innovative. I remember Speedy during his farming days. He was one of the biggest farmers on the Eastern Shore of Maryland, but he was very innovative as well. He was always looking for an advantage. One of the things he did that was unique was that he had one of the first no till planters on the coast. It was homemade and had different fabricated parts on it. My dad loved to farm, and he ran that planter for Speedy as much as he could. They used to go all over with that planter because it was the only one around. Walt was the same way. He was very innovative mechanically. He was definitely a Kenny Weld type of guy who could drive a race car and come up with unique ideas to make the cars faster. The two were really more like a father and son than friends.*

Through all the dirt track success and experience building cars for dirt track racing, it would not be long before Speedy had aspirations to enter racing's biggest stage. In the early 1970s, Speedy started to field a car in NASCAR for the likes of Paul Tyler, Toby Tobias, Kenny Brightbill, Bobby Isaac, Johnny Rutherford and Ramo Stott. The team had their biggest successes at NASCAR's biggest event of the year, the Daytona 500. In 1974, with Ramo Stott driving the Smithville Farms Chevrolet, the team finished an impressive third, running against teams with much larger budgets and greater experience. Mike Reed remembers that race well.

> *Even though winning the pole at Daytona was a big deal, I think Speedy was proudest of their third-place finish in the race in 1974. He was very happy that day. It was the first race out for the new Chevrolet and was the very first brand-new car Speedy had bought for NASCAR. It was a Hutcherson-Pagan chassis. That was the also last race with big-block power before NASCAR went to small-blocks.*

One might think it was beginner's luck for a small team to finish third in front of many of NASCAR's biggest teams in NASCAR's biggest race; however, Speedy and his team proved everyone wrong by returning the following year and finishing fifth in the 1975 Daytona 500. In the 1976 race, Ramo Stott put the car on the pole with an average speed of 183.356 miles per hour, putting the small town of Smithville and Speedy Reed on the map

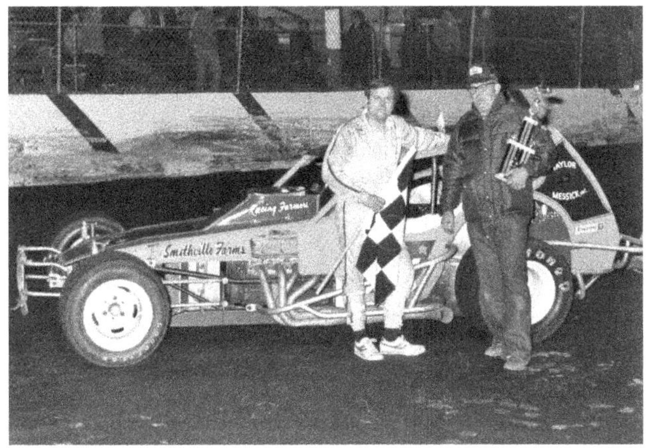

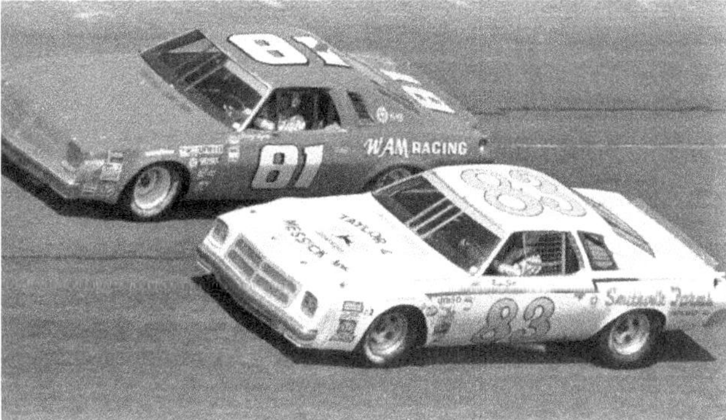

Top: Driver Walt Breeding in Victory Lane with owner Norris "Speedy" Reed and his Kenny Weld Chassis Modified. *Courtesy of Becky Reed.*

Left: The no. 83 car driven by Ramo Stott and owned by Norris "Speedy" Reed leads the field to the start of the 1976 Daytona 500. *Courtesy of Becky Reed.*

and in the NASCAR history books forever. The team finished in twenty-sixth place that day after a blown engine ended their hopes of a Daytona win. Speedy Reed will forever be known as the friendly farmer from Smithville, Maryland, who helped so many racers in the area and eventually climbed his way to the top of the sport doing things his way. His dream of racing in the Daytona 500 was a great example to everyone that hard work pays off and that, if you can dream it, you can do it.

6
BILL LAWSON

When a young Bill Lawson was a member of the Delaware Stock Car Racing Association—at the time, run by George Reed—in the early 1960s, he often attended races at US 13 Speedway. At the second race run at the speedway in 1966, no one showed up to flag the race. Bill remembers, "I was at the time what you would call a pit steward. George came up to me and said, 'Bill, I want you to flag.' I climbed up in the flagging stand, and twenty-eight years later I climbed out. I just never stopped. I flagged Delmar, Harrington Fair, Little Lincoln, Airport and Georgetown Speedways. I was flagging two, three or four tracks a weekend." Racing roots run deep in the Lawson family, and Bill credits his father, Clifford Lawson, who was the president of the Delaware Stock Car Racing Association in the 1950s, for helping him find his love of racing. Bill remembers those early years of racing in Delaware.

My first race was at the old Boots Wilkins race track across from the Starting Gate on Route 9. I was six years old when I attended my first race there, and with Dad being as deeply involved in racing as he was I just fell in love with racing. Now, I have a grandson involved in racing so that is four generations of Lawsons that have been involved with racing. I went with my dad to all the old tracks in Pocomoke, Magnolia, Sandtown and Love Creek, which are all now gone. We started out at Boots Wilkins track until Melvin Joseph built his track in 1949. Boots track went back to horse

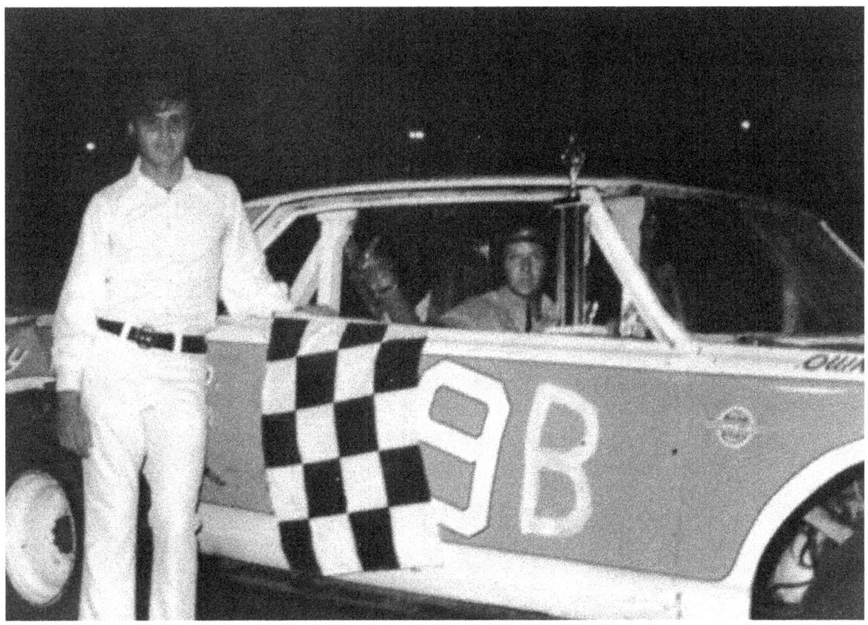

Driver Richard Dix is congratulated by flagman Bill Lawson at Little Lincoln Speedway. *Courtesy of Betty Wyatt-Dix.*

> *racing, and we went to the new track at Georgetown. We were there every Friday night, and I mean every one. I was there every Friday night until September of 1960 when I went into the service.*

Anyone who had the privilege of being able to see Bill flag a race witnessed one of the most unique flagging styles in all of racing. Bill's signature style of throwing one leg over the railing of the flag stand and leaning precariously out over the track was certainly attention grabbing. Bill explains how he came up with his signature style.

> *It was just a deal where I was flagging and I wanted to reward the winner. At Delmar Speedway with the flag stand down near the track, I could get real close to the cars. So, as the winner of a particular race would come down the speedway to take the checkered flag, I would lean over and pop them on the roof of the car with my flag and they would know they were the winner. The thing of it is if you just stand there and twirl your flags, to me, you have not rewarded a racer that has busted their butt and won the race. I just wanted to give them some recognition, and a flagman can do that.*

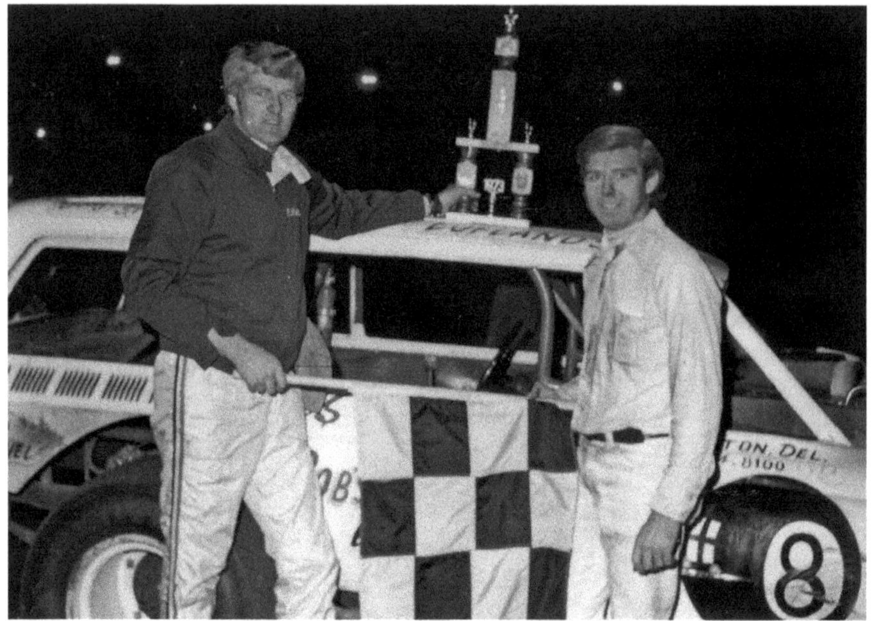

Flagman Bill Lawson congratulates feature winner Eddie Pettyjon in 1973. *Courtesy of the Pettyjohn family.*

With thousands of miles of racing under his flag, Bill had only a few close calls during his career. The worst was one night at Delmar, Delaware. "At Delmar, one night, Richard Jarvis got tapped by another car on the left rear. It was just a racing incident. There was no bad intention on the other driver. But when that car came around and hit the fence, it came right through the stand. Boards went everywhere, the flags went everywhere and I was laying in the middle of it all." Bill humorously adds to the story. "A funny moment happened after the incident. An intoxicated spectator came over to me as I was laying on the ground and said, 'If you would have thrown the yellow light on, that wouldn't have happened.' I just could have wrung his neck at that time!"

Conducting himself with the utmost professionalism was always a priority for Bill when he flagged. He remembers how another famous flagger influenced his style during his early years in the sport.

> *In the first years that I flagged, I was not as flamboyant, but when I saw some photos of Tex Enright, he was instantly my hero. I styled myself after him. He was always sharp, clean and on the ball. He also drove a race*

> *car, so he had a real keen sense of what was happening on the track, and I learned a lot from that. I flagged from down on the track at Harrington Fair just like Tex did at Flemington Speedway up in New Jersey. My style of flagging was a direct result of emulating him. We even became really good friends. We would call each other up and chat about racing as well as visiting each other often.*

One would think, flagging in a close-knit area like Delaware, that Bill would eventually have had a confrontation with one of the racers while controlling and flagging the race, but his professionalism always kept otherwise tense situations in check.

> *I knew every driver out there, their family and kids. I had a connection with every one of those drivers. I could tell them to buzz off and then go drink a beer with them later that night. That's the way we were. We did not carry things over from week to week. When I finished talking to a driver, if we had a problem, I felt very confident that our relationship was as strong or stronger than when we started the conversation.*

So great were Bill's contributions to the sport of racing that in March 2018, Georgetown Speedway dedicated the flagstand at the speedway in his honor. As with Bill finding the love of racing through his father, Clifford, Bill's sons carry on the family tradition of being at the track on

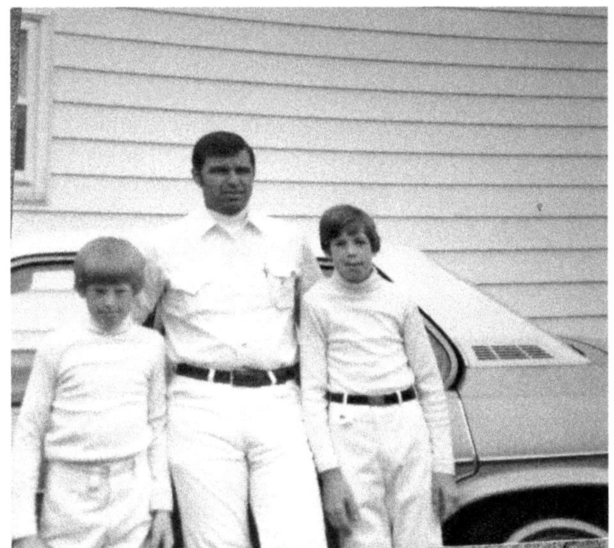

Always the consummate showman, flagman Bill Lawson (*center*) heads to Georgetown looking sharp with his helpers and sons Opie Lawson (*left*) and Kirk Lawson (*right*). *Courtesy of the Lawson family.*

a weekly basis. Bill's late son Chris "Opie" Lawson was a flagman for the World Karting Association up and down the East Coast, making him the third generation of Lawsons to wave a flag at a racetrack. Bill's other son, Kirk, is also heavily involved in racing. Kirk has flagged at Georgetown Speedway and is a successful and competitive diver in the Little Lincoln Race Car Series. With Kirk's son, Robby Lawson, now racing quarter midgets, it looks like the Lawson name will be involved in Delaware racing for the foreseeable future.

7
EDDIE PETTYJOHN

You cannot talk about racing in the First State without mentioning the name Pettyjohn. Eddie Pettyjohn and the Pettyjohn family have been at the forefront of racing in Delaware since its beginnings. Eddie had a keen interest in racing since he was a small child, when his dad, William Pettyjohn, helped build Georgetown Speedway for his brother-in-law, Melvin Joseph.

> *I was like four years old when I started going to the races. During my preteen years, I would sneak under the fence to get inside the pits at Georgetown Speedway. I remember those early racers like Johnny Martin, Horace Williams, Phil Gemendon, Leon Manchester and Johnny Stoltzfus. I just had a vision in my head and there was no doubt what I was going to do. In school, they would ask me what I wanted to do, and I just told them I was going to drive a race car.*

And drive a race car Pettyjohn did. With well over four hundred race wins at many different tracks in many different types of race cars, Pettyjohn's career spanned decades and went from the dirt tracks to the asphalt speedways of NASCAR.

Pettyjohn took his first laps around the track at Georgetown when Snookie Vent let him try his car on the speedway for practice. Needless to say, Pettyjohn's talent to pilot a race car was obvious to everyone who saw him.

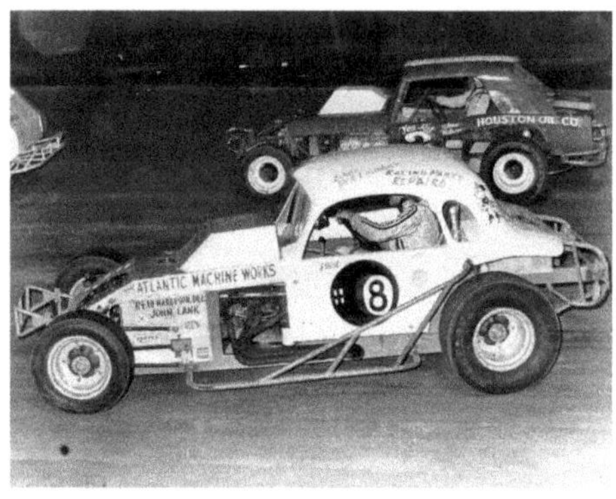

Eddie Pettyjohn proved to be one of the area's most versatile drivers, winning in several classes over the years. *Courtesy of Melvin Joseph Jr.*

> *In the beginning, we ran Little Lincoln and the old quarter mile track at Delmar. I ran my own car no. 8 at Little Lincoln and Harry Dutton's no. 88 at Delmar. Dutton's car was red with his no. 88 on the side. It kind of had a wing painted on the side. My uncle Melvin Joseph's car always had the no. 49 with the wing painted on the side so we decided to go with the no. 88 and wing. In my own car, I started running the no. 8 and somewhere down the line I had a bunch of friends who liked to shoot pool downtown so the number became 8 ball."*

One of his first actual race cars came from a unique situation. "My friend, Jason Wyatt, had a fifty-seven Chevrolet street car, and we were going down a road with a lot of curves in it and he was driving and I was riding. Well! He turned it upside down around one of the corners and that became my race car. We brought it back to my shop and made it into a race car."

Pettyjohn was not only a great driver but also an excellent mechanic, as evidenced by this early story from Delmar.

> *One night we were racing at Delmar in my own car and the track was on the other side of the dragstrip. They told me I could not run because I had the steering in the middle of the car. I used to run it in the middle because I felt safer in the center of the car instead of by the door. They told me I was illegal, and we had been winning quite a few races at the time so I guess they thought that was an unfair advantage. Well, don't you know that the lights were on the dragstrip next to the speedway that night and a plane thought it was an airport landing strip and tried to land. He came down and pulled back up after realizing he made a big mistake. When he did, he clipped some power lines, he was so low. Well, while the lights were out, we took off and went to a service station south of the Delaware/Maryland*

line and asked the guy if he could do some welding for us. He said no, but there was a torch and welder in the shop, and we were welcome to use them. So, we cut the seat out of the floor and moved it back to the left and moved the steering wheel back to the original location. We sped back to Delmar just as they were finishing repairs to the lights. We showed them the changes, went out on the track and won the feature race!

After a successful career driving everything from Late Models, Modifieds and NASCAR Grand National race cars, Pettyjohn says his favorite car was also the fan favorite, the 8-ball Corvair Station Wagon that was so dominant in its day.

The wagon was the most comfortable car I ever drove. I could sit in the middle, have my right foot on the gas on the passenger side and the brake on the left side. It had a Mustang seat in it with a pipe welded on the side of it. We built that car from scratch in the shop. It was just a great car to drive. I would use the heel of my hand and drive it like it had a suicide knob on it. I would go in those corners and that car would just sit so pretty.

Pettyjohn's legacy of driving excellence ranges from his favorite win at the Fairgrounds at the Delaware State Fair in Harrington to his top-ten NASCAR finish at Dover International Speedway, a stunning career that

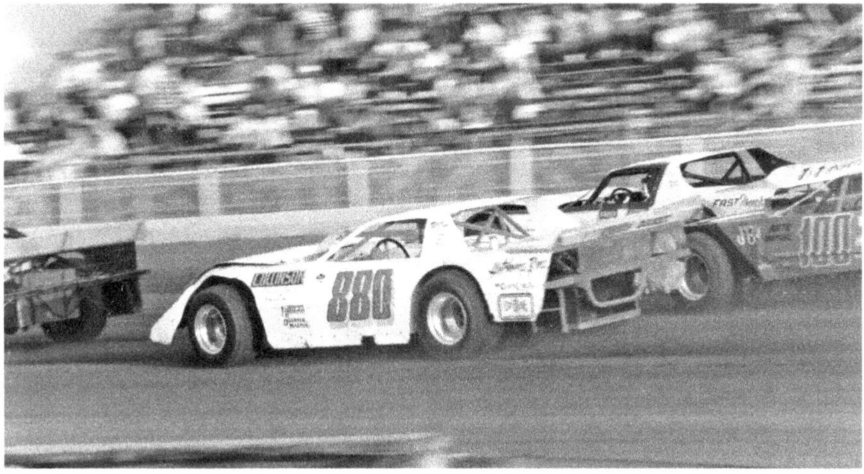

Eddie Pettyjohn in the no. 880 Hitchens Trucking Company Late Model makes it three wide at the 1985 Delaware State Fair race. *Courtesy of Don and Linda Allen, D&L Photos.*

fans still talk about to this day. The Pettyjohns' legacy continues, as all of his sons have gone on to become successful drivers in their own right. Kenny Pettyjohn, David Pettyjohn and Mark Pettyjohn have all found success on Delaware's speedways and beyond. Still today, if you happen to drive through downtown Milton, Delaware, you will see a small garage with a race car or race cars being worked on within its walls, as has been the case for decades. There is still an 8-ball race car in the shop, and the sounds of sheet metal being cut and race cars being worked on fill the air. With the family still involved in racing, it looks like the Pettyjohn name will be associated with racing in Delaware for some time, just as it should be.

8

JACK SAPP

1932-2014

Jack Sapp's introduction to auto racing can be traced to his time as a young man hanging around and working at Jack Fitzgerald's junkyard as well as at Doug Morgan's shop, which at the time fielded cars for Johnny Martin. Hanging around racers, car owners and mechanics, it was only a matter of time before Sapp made his first start driving a race car. Sapp, who always drove for other owners in his long career, got his start driving a car for Jack Fitzgerald in the Hobby class, beginning a lifelong love of all things racing.

The list of owners that Sapp drove for in his career is indeed impressive. In no particular order, some of the owners and teams Sapp drove include the following: Jack Fitzgerald, Doug Morgan, Earl Ridley, Harry Dutton, Jake Twilley, Marshall Baker, Cabbage Corner Race Team, the Abshers, George Adams, Everett Messick and Jim Grahm. In that long line of owners, Sapp's car numbers included 97, 9A, 17, 29, 90, 56 and GO.

Jack's son and racer, Bobby Sapp, remembers his dad's career fondly and says Jack enjoyed racing at all the tracks where he competed but believes his dad enjoyed racing at Delaware's Little Lincoln Speedway the most.

> *I would say he probably enjoyed the days racing at Little Lincoln the most, racing those '55 and '57 Chevys. That was when the average man could afford a race car. I remember one night we tore the front end up on the race car in the heat race and we simply drove across the road to Fitzgerald's Junkyard, took parts off the car in the junkyard to fix the car and still be out on the track to race the feature.*

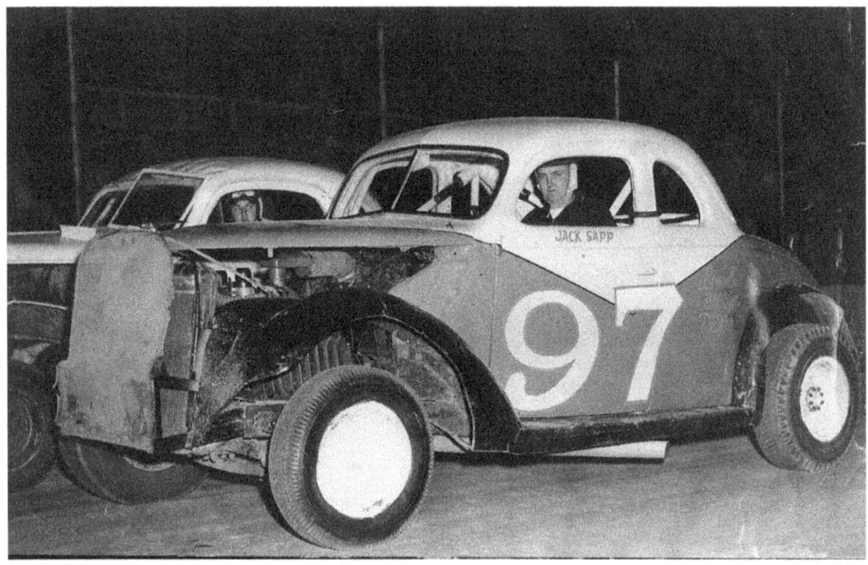

From racing early coupes to modern-day Modifieds, Jack Sapp was a winner. *Courtesy of Bobby Sapp.*

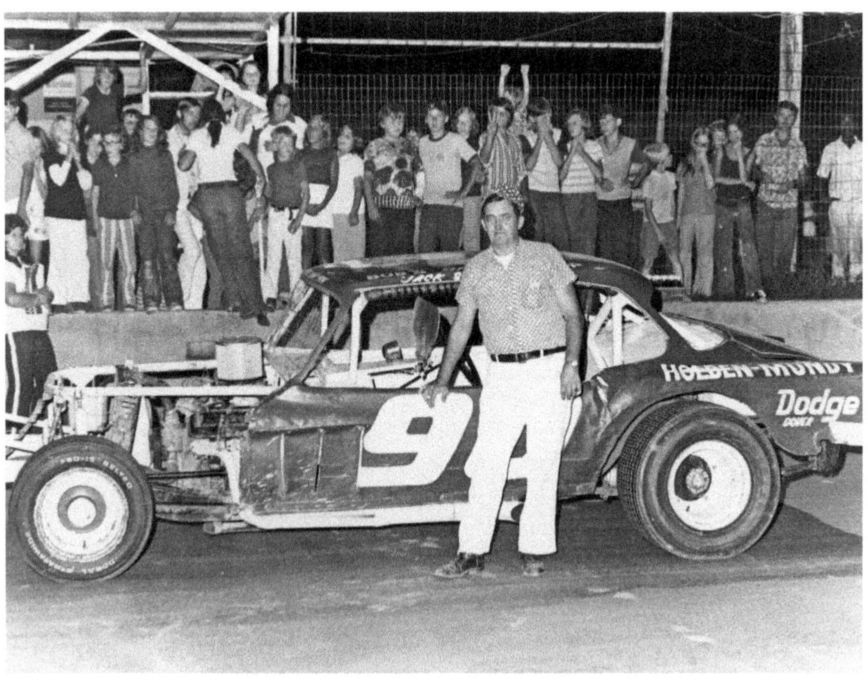

Kids line up along the fence to get a view of feature winner Jack Sapp and his famous polka-dotted cap. *Courtesy of Charlie Brown.*

Most fans remember Sapp and his crew showing up to the tracks in their distinctive red-and-white polka-dotted caps and uniforms. Bobby explains how the trend got started.

> *It was a welder's cap he had. I do not have a clue where he got that hat, but he just started wearing it to the track and everyone started poking at him about it. So, for the heck of it, everyone on the team got one and stated wearing them. Then, a lady in Lincoln, Delaware, started making shirts for everyone, so we all started showing up in red and white polka dots from head to toe. It was something we never planned. It just kind of happened.*

Sapp was a racer's racer. Knowing all aspects of the car, Sapp was dedicated to making sure the team was as successful as it could be, even if that meant long hours in the shop, as Bobby Sapp explains.

> *Dad loved Georgetown Speedway as well. He really enjoyed all the tracks. I remember one time back when Walt Breeding was promoting Georgetown. Dad wrecked the car bad at US 13 Speedway on Saturday night, and Georgetown was running a special show on Sunday, and if I am not mistaken, it was twin fifty-lap features. The car was torn up bad. It was really the beginning of the Tobias-style cars and we were running a copy of one of those cars. I remember Vaughn Morgan making copies of those cars at the time as well as Walt Breeding. Dad and the crew stayed up all night getting the car back together and went out and won both of the features! Dad said he was so tired that he had to put his hand on his knee to push the brake pedal down to stop the car. This was back when there was no power steering. He was spent after that day. That track was so fast and intense, it was amazing he was able to perform like that on very limited rest.*

Sapp's most successful times came toward the end of his long career. In 1981, at fifty-six years of age, Sapp won nine times. The last race Sapp ever won was in the very competitive and now-defunct MODCAR series. On July 19, 1984, Sapp won the last MODCAR race held at Delaware International Speedway, beating out the top Modified talent of that period.

As with most racing families, the Sapp family racing bug spans generations. Jack's son Bobby got his first start in a Modified in the same no. GO car that his father drove. It was a case of being in the right place at the right time, according to Bobby.

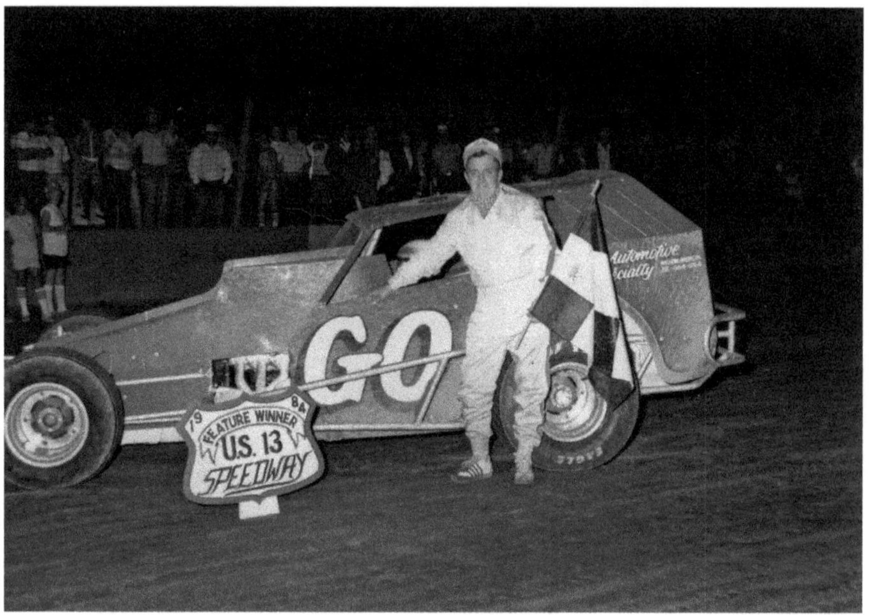

Jack Sapp in Victory Lane during the 1984 racing season. *Courtesy of Don and Linda Allen, D&L Photos.*

> *The owner of that car lived in Harrington, and I lived on Route 14 between Milford and Harrington. He was driving the car on the road, and I saw him slow way down and then take off. He did this several times, and about the third time he did it I called him up and asked him "What in the world are you doing, stopping in front of my house and then taking off?" He said that he needed someone to help work on this race car and nobody will help me. He had a driver, but no one was helping him work on the car. I told him I would work on the race car if I could drive it! He told me to "come on over and get started helping me then." That's how I got the ride in that car. I drove from 1987 to 1997. My son Nick was starting to get involved racing Karts, and it was time for me to help him, just like my dad helped me.*

Jack Sapp's grandson Nick Sapp continues the Sapp family tradition to this day, racing highly competitive wingless Micro Sprints at Bridgeport Speedway. When Bobby and Nick load up the trailer, Jack Sapp's racing spirit goes with them. As a tribute to the family patriarch, you will find hanging in the corner of the race car trailer Jack Sapp's last polka-dotted hat, which still travels to every race with them, reminding them of past glory and future victories.

9
THE WHITE FAMILY

Racing in Delaware has always been a family-based sport. Just take a walk through the pits at your next visit to the speedway, and you will see past generations of racers helping out current drivers set up and work on their cars. Often, there will be young children playing next to the family trailer with toy cars on a carved-out dirt track they made, dreaming of their turn behind the wheel. No family symbolizes this lifelong love of racing better than the White family. For over five generations, the White family has been involved in some form of racing in and around Delaware. Current racer Tim White explains the family's love of racing, how it all got started and where the family race car no. 16 originated.

> *We have always just been involved in the sport in some way as long as I can remember. My grandfather Freddie White was the first one to race in the family. He raced all along the eastern shore. He drove a car that was numbered "Sweet 16." My dad, Dave White, was asked one time where he got his number from, and I remember him telling the people that his dad had a car lettered "Sweet 16," and he liked that 16 number so much he just decided to run it for the whole time he owned and raced his cars.*

Dave White was a fixture in the early Eight-Cylinder and Late Model classes at Delaware International Speedway and Georgetown Speedway. Dave took the love of racing he inherited from his father and carved out a path of excellence for his family to follow through the years. Dave White won

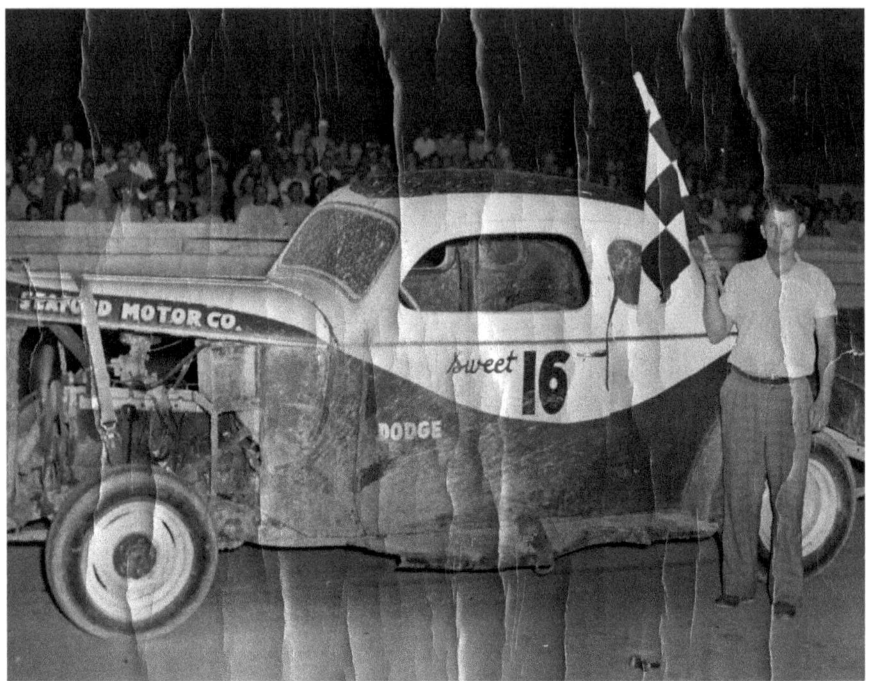

This old tattered photo shows the "Sweet 16" of Freddie White picking one of the first wins in a long history of success for the White family. *Courtesy of Louis O'Neal.*

the Delaware International Speedway (then named US 13 Speedway) Track Championship in 1969, 1970 and 1975. He also proved his excellence at the slightly larger Georgetown Speedway by winning its track championship in 1978. Obviously, hanging around the track had quite the impression on a young child, and Dave's three sons were no exception. It was not long before the third generation of Whites began showing up at the track with their own no. 16 car to race. The first one to jump in a car and put the no. 16 in Victory Lane was David White Jr., more popularly known as "Bunky." Bunky mostly ran Limited Late Models and also dabbled in the Street Stock and Econo Mod classes. Not far behind, his brother Tim got bit by the racing bug as well. Winning the first Street Modified Championship at Delaware International Speedway in 1985 early in his career started Tim down a successful path in many aspects of motorsports.

> *After starting off in the Street Modified and winning the championship in 1985, I jumped into the Limited Late Models in 1986. After winning one race, I blew the motor and really just could not afford the cost of*

> *racing at that point in my life. It was just one thing after another, and that's when a series of events led me to become a pit crew member in NASCAR. I was very lucky to have been involved with those teams at that time in history. I was able to crew for the likes of Darrell Waltrip, Ricky Rudd, Stacy Compton, Dick Trickle, Ron Hornaday and Phil Parsons. When I was with Rudd, we won the Brickyard 400, Phoenix, Martinsville and Dover races. With Waltrip, I was on the winning crew when he won the Daytona 500. It was just an incredible experience to be part of those teams at that time.*

After seizing his opportunities in the NASCAR community, Tim eventually returned to his Delaware roots and started to run Dwarf cars with his nephew Sparky White. What was intended to be just a fun thing to do on his off weekends from NASCAR turned into much more. The Dwarf car division eventually morphed into the Modified Lites Division, and Tim found his stride in the class, winning two Delaware International Track Championships in 2006 and 2015, bringing his total championships to three, equaling his father, Dave White. The third White brother, Kevin, also kept the family tradition in racing going strong, as he decided to try winged Sprint Car racing with the United Racing Club (URC), the nation's oldest touring racing group.

After such a long career in racing, one might think that Tim White would be ready to back away from the sport. But Tim sees no end in sight for his racing career. "As long as I can climb through the window, hold a steering wheel and have fun, I am going to race," he says. And why not? The fourth generation of the White family is establishing its own legacy on the track. Son of Bunky White, David White III, otherwise known as "Sparky," is having much success in the Crate Late Model class, as evidenced by his winning the 2016 Delaware International Speedway Crate Late Model Championship for car owners Tommy and Debbie Elliott. Sparky's brother Matt is involved in racing as well, competing in the always entertaining Little Lincoln Class. As if four generations of winning racers were not enough, members of the fifth generation of Whites involved in racing are already honing their skills. Sparky White's two young sons, Landon and Chase White, are currently running and winning races at the Club Milton Speedway, gaining in both knowledge and experience. One day, they too might be able to race at the same tracks as have their family members. It's a great legacy, as Tim White explains.

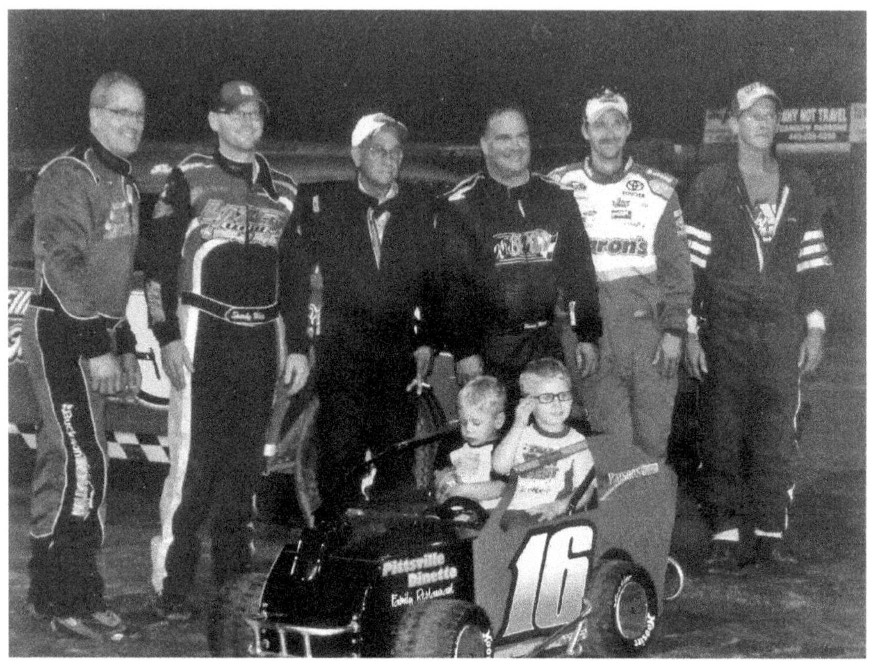

The Racing White family are, *from left to right*: Tim White, Sparky White, Dave White, Kevin White, Matt White and Bunky White. Seated in the car are Chase and Landon White. *Courtesy of Tim White.*

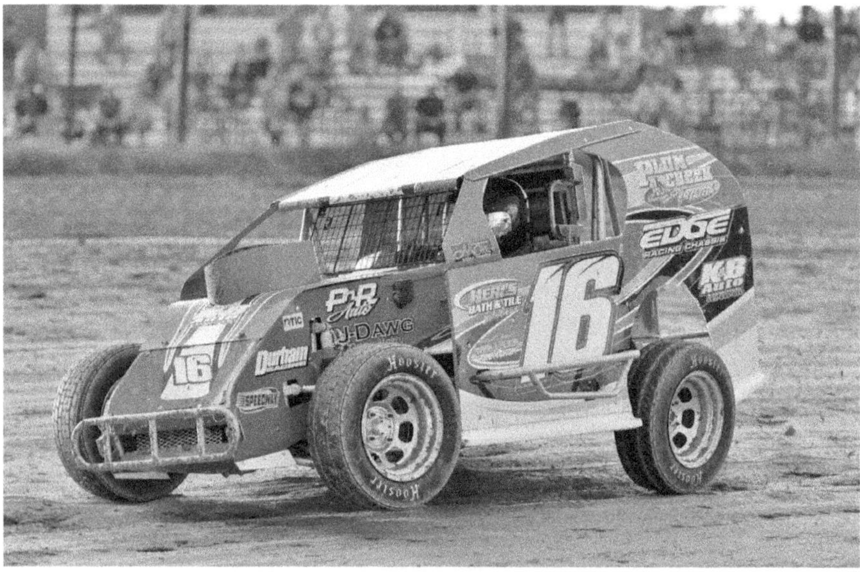

Tim White finds some bite and lifts the left front tire toward the sky at Delaware International Speedway. *Courtesy of Landstone Photography.*

For five generations, we have pictures of the no. 16 sitting in Victory Lane. We even have a photo of my mom, Lou, winning a powder-puff race back in the day behind the wheel of the no. 16. Nine different family members have won races, and we all did it in the no. 16. This year, Landon won the championship at Club Milton driving the no. 16, so we are very thankful for our past success and we are definitely looking forward to what is in store for the White family in the future.

10

WALT BREEDING

1946–2018

Rarely does a person have such wide-ranging influence and impact on a sport as Walt Breeding did. Driver, inventor, master fabricator, builder, businessman, promoter and mentor are just some of the many titles Breeding had throughout his busy life in racing. Like most future racers, Breeding got his start racing karts. He explained his early influences in racing in an interview conducted before his passing in 2018.

> *I started in go-karts like most other people. My grandfather gave me a go-kart in 1957 for my twelfth birthday. The karting craze had just gotten big on the East Coast. There was a go-kart track over in Cambridge, Maryland, down by the Moose Club, and that is where we started racing. I always had a passion for cars and just worked my way up from the karts to the full-size cars. I also started out working on the Smithfield Farms Modified of Norris "Speedy" Reed when I was twelve years old. I used to ride my bicycle down the road three or four miles to help work on the cars and do whatever they needed. That relationship would become instrumental in my racing career, because it gave me a chance to really get involved with everything that racing was about. I started building cars my senior year in high school. I built a Sedan to run at Reading Fairgrounds in the Modified division. That was our first Modified we ran and was numbered as no. 141. Leon Manchester had a special '55 Chevy frame they had built, and I used that to build the car from scratch. That was a big learning experience for me.*

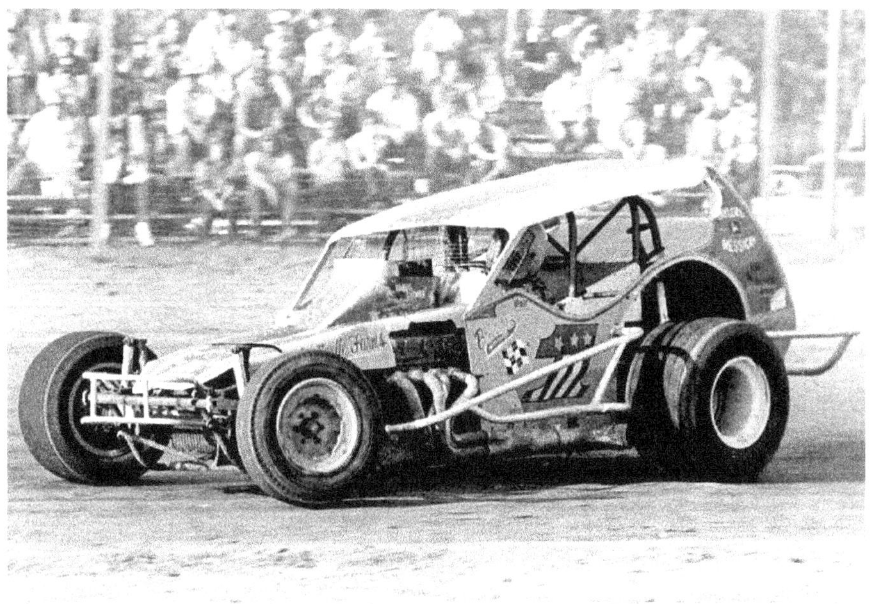

Walt Breeding behind the wheel of one of the most unique Modifieds ever: the Kenny Weld offset car. *Courtesy of Becky Reed.*

Breeding would gain valuable experience as a car builder well before he ever thought of getting behind the wheel of a race car himself.

> *I didn't drive anything for a right good while. I was building cars hot and heavy there at the beginning and I just made up my mind I did not want to drive until I was ready. I wanted to make sure I had all the pieces of the puzzle lined up in order to be competitive. I also wanted to drive my own car that I built. I drove the first year for myself, and the second year I ran for Howard Davis as the team car to Haines Tull, who drove the no. 3D. I drove that car for two years then moved on from there to drive the familiar no. 1 Taylor & Messick sponsored Modified.*

During his ten-year driving career, Breeding piloted mostly cars he built himself. The one exception was the radically offset designed Modified that was built by racing legend Kenny Weld. "Norris 'Speedy' Reed wanted to get something different. We had our cars and Speedy just decided we should try something new. Weld was frustrated with the newly designed car and asked us if we wanted to try out this new design, and we said, 'sure.' Weld did not have much success with that offset style car, but we got it

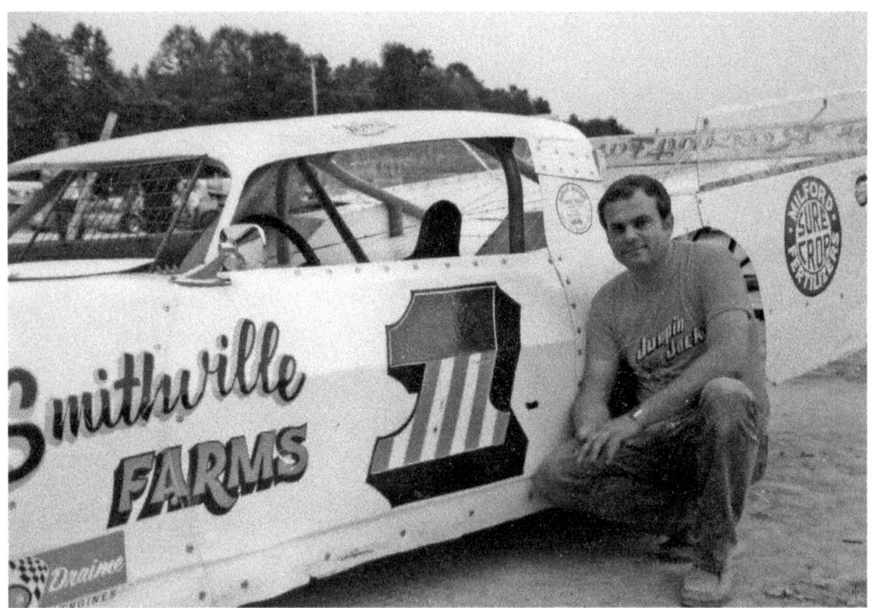

Walt Breeding, next to the Smithville Farms no. 1, was equally comfortable behind the wheel of a Late Model or Modified. *Courtesy of Don and Linda Allen, D&L Photos.*

dialed in and had great success with it. It was a challenge to drive, but that car was so fast."

Throughout his driving career, Breeding still found time to build race cars and even help his friend Speedy Reed dive into the highly competitive NASCAR series. Breeding continued to win races and have great success up and down the East Coast in both Modifieds and Late Models until stepping away from driving for good to concentrate on the business of building race cars. The decision to leave driving came to Breeding while racing on the track one night.

> *I wanted to stay in business after I quit driving. I really started to think about that after I got hurt in a race at Delmar. It made me realize I had to give up something. I had driven for ten years and I was happy with what I had accomplished. I had three businesses at the time, and I wanted to keep making a living, and after getting hurt that one time I just could never really come to terms with that. Normally, I was in the car and I was pumped and hyper-focused on what the car was doing and where I was going to go next, but that incident put things in perspective for me. I never planned on it, but I was racing at Delmar one night and the caution came out for a wreck and*

> *as I drove around the wreck, I just said to myself, "You know what, I don't need to do this anymore," and I just pulled the car into the pits and quit. I never intended to, but that's how it happened. Of course, the crew was asking what was wrong with the car, but there was nothing wrong, it was just my time to bow out.*

Along with his innovative Modified chassis and Kart chassis that carried the Bandit brand name, Breeding also was successful in bringing Dwarf cars and Mod Lights to the area. The smaller but more affordable cars carried a new name for Breeding. Pro Race Cars was a huge success for Breeding, and his innovative designs and ability to organize a sanctioning body for the class led to the class's success not only in Delaware but also across the nation.

Sadly, Walt Breeding succumbed to cancer early in 2018. His innovative spirit and countless contributions to racing live on and are remembered by all in the racing community. Always optimistic and pushing the envelope, Breeding enjoyed racing until his last days. Partnering with several friends, Breeding constructed two radically different designed Modifieds in the last years of his life. If you were lucky enough to have a conversation with him during that time and mention the cars, he would enthusiastically tell you all about the design and how the cars should work on the track. The spark in his eyes was contagious. You could see those mechanical genius wheels

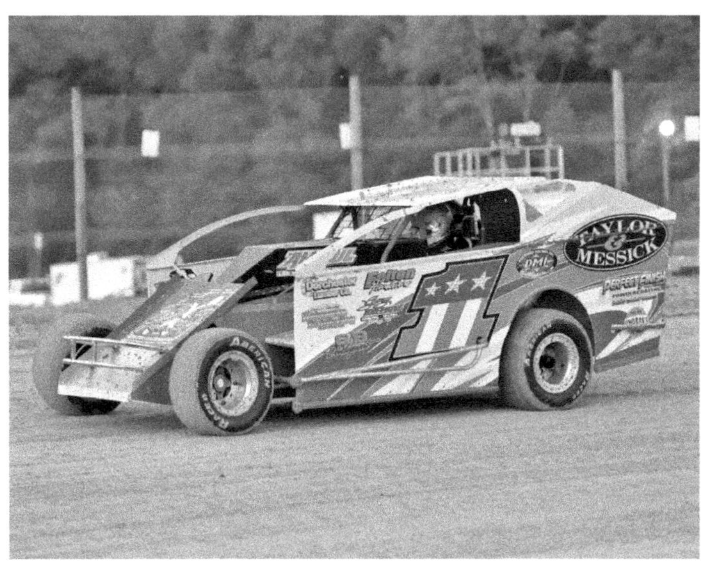

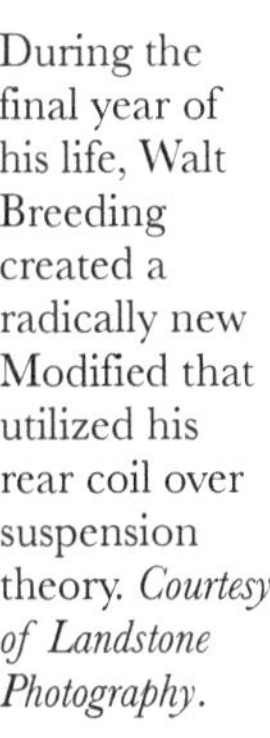

During the final year of his life, Walt Breeding created a radically new Modified that utilized his rear coil over suspension theory. *Courtesy of Landstone Photography.*

turning in his head, always looking forward, pushing the envelope and challenging the status quo. Breeding could not look at a race car without wanting to improve on its design and make it better, and he will always be remembered for his drive and determination to do so.

11

CHARLIE CATHELL

The Cathell family has long been a staple of racing in the First State. The family-owned Delaware International Speedway has been Delaware's longest continually running racetrack since its inaugural season in 1965. Although the drag strip got its start in 1963, it was not until 1965 that turning left and racing in circles caught on. From 1965 to the present day, the facility has been owned by the Cathell family. Started by Charlie Cathell's parents, Bill and Juanita Cathell, the facility has continuously hosted weekly racing longer than any other facility in Delaware. In an era when tracks are closing at an alarming rate due to rising property costs, overdevelopment and poor track management, Delaware International Speedway has thrived, remaining a historic example of what grassroots racing is all about. Its success is a testament to the vision and hard work of the Cathell family. Current promoter Charlie Cathell remembers the speedway's humble beginnings and how the whole thing came about.

> *As a high school student that weighed 103 pounds during my senior year, my sports activities were limited. Football was something we all liked to play, but I found out I was not really big enough to play that, and I was just okay at baseball. So, I indulged myself into auto mechanics in high school, which led to me racing go-karts. When I was about thirteen or fourteen, we would race our kart that we built ourselves at a track in Newark, Maryland. That's how we started in racing. I would use that kart during the week to go to work. My mother's side of the family were farmers.*

I would change the gearing on the go-kart and travel the seven miles from my house to the farm to work. When it was time to race on the weekend, I would change the gearing on the kart and go racing. As that progressed and I got my license, we started to street race. We had some pretty quick Fords back then, and I just loved the thrill of competition. I often joke with people it was cheaper to build a drag strip than pay the fines from street racing. My dad was a raw products manager at Delaney Foods and had a small trucking company. Looking back, he was a pretty smart guy in being able to get things done when you did not have anything to start with in the first place. My parents had progressed in life to where they were looking to get involved in something new. They looked at a business venture in Ocean City and a car dealership, but both fell through. So, then we got thinking since we like racing maybe we should think about building a drag strip. We had a piece of property picked out by the airport and were almost ready to settle, but at the last meeting with the county officials, they asked us what day we intended to run on. When we told them Sunday, they said that I guess we understood that in this county we could not charge anyone to get in. We were shocked! They said because of the blue law the only thing that could be open and charge money on a Sunday were pharmacies and movie theaters. So, that was the end of that location. At the time, I was working for Perdue in their settlement department when a good friend told me about a piece of property that he wanted to sell. That ended up being the location where the track is today. There was no access to U.S. 13 from the property. You had to enter from 13A, the old Delmar Road. It was all farm property. We then bought a forty-foot piece of the adjoining property so we could access U.S. 13 as well.

Construction of the dragway started soon after the property was purchased. Charlie remembers what a struggle it was just to open the doors for business, as not everything went according to plan during the construction.

The drag strip was supposed to open in June of 1963, but it got pushed back to August. We had problems with the track. Dad was driving down the track in March and got about halfway down the strip and the car went right through the surface. We had invested so much to get to that point and now we had a major issue with the track. It was a mess because we had already invested so much financially, and the track collapsed. Well, the asphalt company said "It's not our fault; it's a base problem." The grading contractor said, "I had your guy get on our grader and check it out before

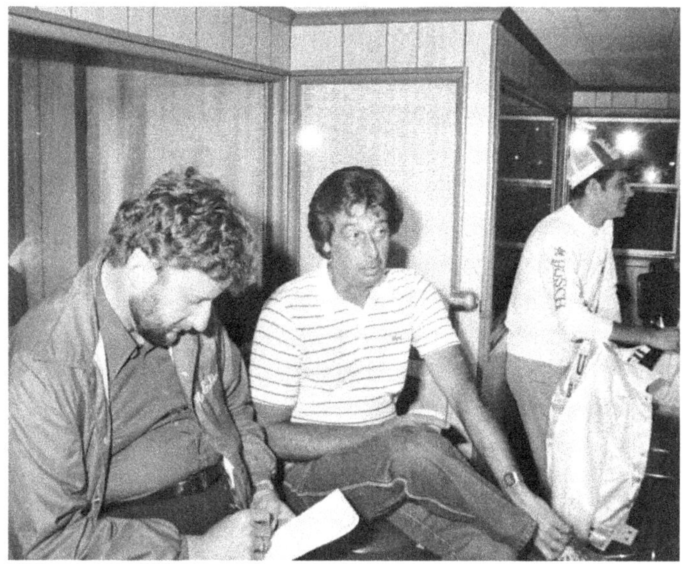

Charlie Cathell (*center*) is interviewed by assistant editor of *Stock Car Racing Magazine*, Herb Dodge (*left*), while Clifford "Biff" Lee (*right*) watches the night's races. *Courtesy of Don and Linda Allen, D&L Photos.*

> *you blacktopped it, so it's not our fault." We could see where this was going. We were going to have to pay for the extensive repairs. We were in a real bind financially, and our bank would not let us borrow any more money because we had already borrowed our max. We went to a banker friend of Dad's, and he told my parents, Bill and Juanita, they had always met every obligation they have ever signed for and that the other banker was right, they would be upside down if they did this, but he was going to take a chance and lend us the money. It was a big chance!*

The big chance taken by the Cathell family started to pay off as word spread about the dragway. In 1965, the dragway welcomed a speedway to the growing motorsports facility.

> *Around 1965, we were approached by a group of owners with the Delaware Auto Racing Association who were looking for a place to race. We built a dirt oval track on the opposite side of the dragway from where the track is now, and the organization leased it from us and ran their own shows. Those real early shows were not really well attended. My dad knew George Bowers, who operated a speedway on the other side of town in the 1950s, really well. He asked him to come out and look at our track and offer suggestions to make it better. Bower's first comment was that the track was too far away from the spectators and the thrill of speed was diminished by this. Plus, he said our car count was minimal. We built a half-mile track.*

He said if we took that same car count and put it on a quarter-mile track, it would look full and the action would be more exciting. So, we made a smaller track inside the half-mile, and the crowds started to show up. Dad also talked to George Bowers and the club about the idea of changing the location of the track to its current location so we could provide a better fan experience and also floated the idea about going to Saturday-night racing so we would not be competing with other tracks who were thirty-five miles away that ran on Fridays. No one said it was a bad idea, but no one really agreed to it either. In the winter of 1969, Dad moved the track to the new location. It was a one-third-mile with a figure-eight track in the middle of it. He got the track all done and decided to run Saturday night, but the organization that organized the races decided they did not want to run races on that night. Dad was crushed and asked me for ideas on what to do. We went to the people that helped us with the drag strip and asked them if they thought we could run the races. Their response was, "Well racing's racing and it can't be that different, our guys race in a straight and those guys turn left, no big deal!" So, we put our heads together and that is when we started to run the whole show. That first show had about seven or eight cars and about thirty to forty people in the stands. We were so let down, but as the

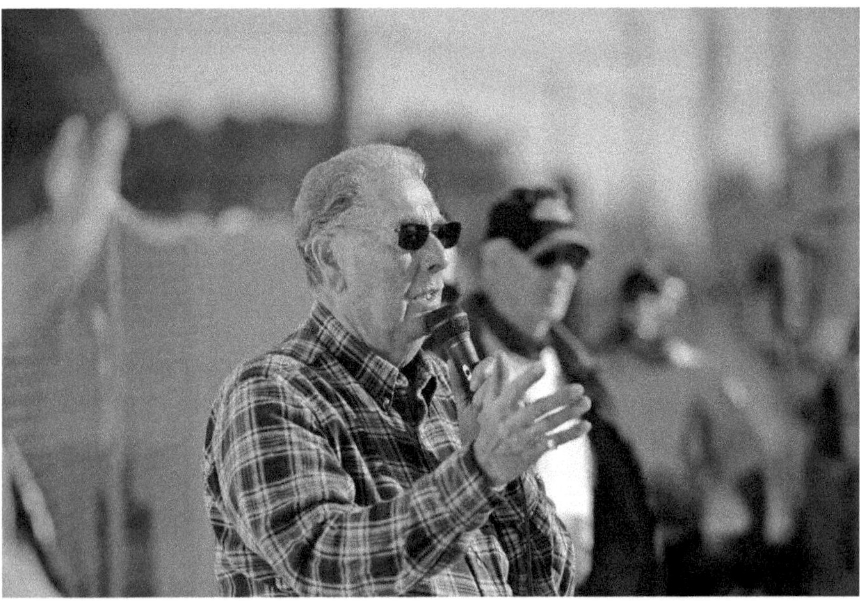

Delaware International Speedway owner and promotor Charlie Cathell addresses drivers before the start of the night's events. *Courtesy of Rick Sweeten Images.*

weeks progressed the association came back to race, but we continued to run things ourselves. That was in 1970. Not long after that, the one-third-mile oval became too small for the car counts. Things just took off, and in 1976, we decided on a weekend just before the Fourth of July to enlarge the track to its current half-mile format. In a two-week period, we moved the drainage ditch by the backstretch, which required state approval, buildings had moved, grandstands had moved, lighting had been moved and the new track was graded and ready to go.

From its humble beginnings, Delaware International Speedway has become a premier motorsports destination and remains Delaware's only weekly dirt track. Over the years, the track has hosted some of the best racers in America and continues its weekly racing tradition. The track also continues to host its two signature events every year: the Camp Barnes Benefit Race, from which all proceeds are donated to the youth camp operated by the Delaware State Police; and the Delaware State Championship races held at the end of each year. Racers and fans alike owe a great deal to the Cathell family for working hard to keep the gates open; if the track was to close, racing in Delaware as we know it could possibly disappear. As one of the hardest-working men in motorsports, Charlie Cathell continues to be a hands-on owner/promoter and is always trying to give the fans and racers more, as evidenced by one of his most unique ideas on track maintenance, the legendary grooming of the track during intermission. Love it or hate it, one has to admire the reasoning behind this unique practice.

I get a lot of complaints about grading the track during intermission, and people say I am trying to sell hot dogs, but I am not making much off of a few extra hot dogs. When my family started this track, I committed myself as a businessperson so that when you buy a ticket and come to see a race, you should be able to see the best possible show we can provide. In that production, there should be a racetrack that is racy. A track that is rough and has a lot of ruts and bumps causes a lot of wrecks that may not be intentional, but the surface just made it so rough the racing was not good. In all my years, I have never seen a rough track smooth itself out on its own. We pride ourselves on taking thirty to forty minutes during intermission to groom the track. I think you will see a much better feature race and the racers will not tear up so much equipment. The fans sometimes give us some grief for grading the track, and I get that. They did not pay to see a grader go around in a circle, but the racers will be the first ones to come tell me that they are glad I smoothed the track out. We try our best to provide the best racing surface possible for the drivers so they can provide the best racing action for the fans.

Next time you see Charlie Cathell at the track, stop for a moment, shake his hand and say thanks for helping to keep racing alive in Delaware. His dedication to providing the best possible facility for local racers and fans is to be appreciated and not taken for granted.

12

SNOOKIE VENT

One of the most colorful characters in all of racing on Delmarva is the legendary Snookie Vent. For years, Snookie's Speed Shop has been a beacon for racers on the East Coast and remains to this day in its original location on Route 1 in Milton, Delaware, still selling parts to racers across the mid-Atlantic. Snookie started his first race in Georgetown in 1959 driving a 1940 Ford Humpback with his familiar no. 86 on the side. The origins of the no. 86 came from Snookie's father-in-law. "My father-in-law drank a right good bit, and his favorite drink was Old Crow 86 Proof. So more often than not when I was working on the race car, he was drinking Old Crow. So, both the no. 86 and the nickname, the Old Crow, got painted on the car, and it kind of stuck."

Before selling parts to racers, Snookie started with a garage in Milton with the help of fellow racer Harry Dutton.

> *I opened a shop right next door to Harry, and people said I had lost my mind. They said I would never get work opening up a shop with Harry Dutton, Harvey Dutton and Bobby Reed right next door. Hell! I had all the work I wanted. If Harry didn't want to do something, he would turn it over to me. If I needed tools, he would send over the tools, and if I didn't know how to do it, he would tell me how to do it. Harry was a great mechanic.*

Snookie remembers those early days of his racing career with a laugh.

> *I ran a hundred lapper one time at Georgetown with an old Ford, and at that time, Georgetown ran the Sportsman and Modified all together at the same time. I was running the Sportsman class and George Harrison was running his old Modified Studebaker, which was much faster. When the racing got through, George came up to me and said, "It's a good thing this was not a two hundred lapper or you would have won the whole thing." Every time George came around to lap me during the race, I would rub his car just a bit with mine, and he jokingly thought I was going to take out the whole field.*

Snookie would eventually make his way to competing in the area's premier racing classes and do quite well, winning many races in a career that spanned decades. While many remember Snookie for his driving, others remember him for his speed shop and all the help he gave local racers. The transition to selling speed parts and working on race cars was an easy one for Snookie. He got into the parts business through racing as a way to race cheaper if he could get the parts at a discount. If one peruses through vintage racing

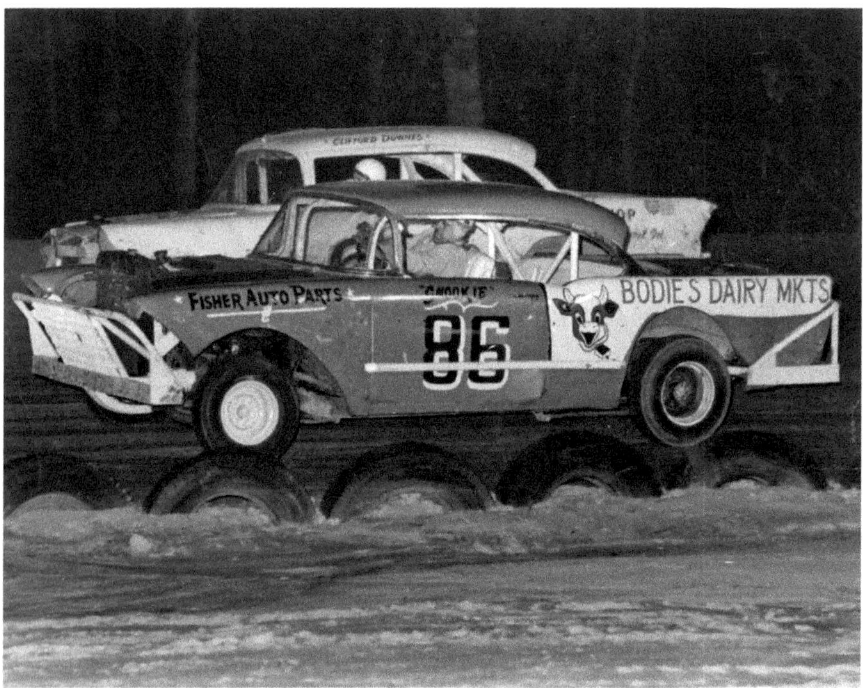

Snookie Vent in the no. 86 at Little Lincoln Speedway. *Courtesy of Snookie Vent.*

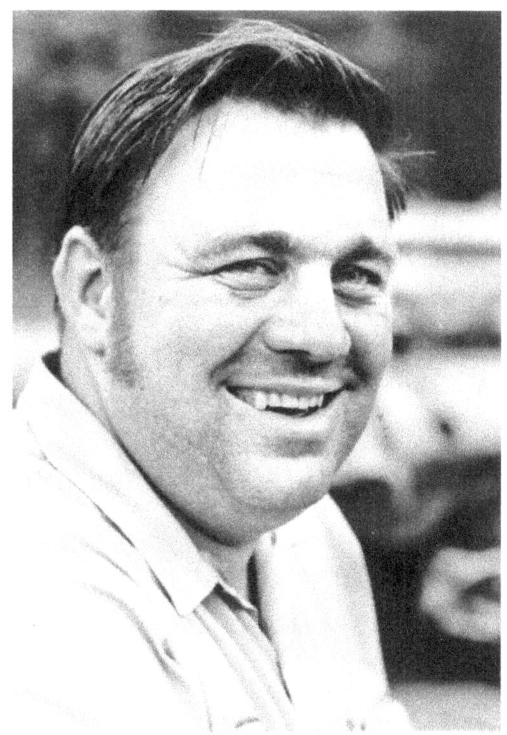

Left: Driver and owner of the legendary speed shop, Snookies Speed Parts, the "Old Crow" Snookie Vent. *Courtesy of Snookie Vent.*

Below: Snookie Vent posing in Victory Lane after a hard-fought win in his Modified. *Courtesy of Snookie Vent.*

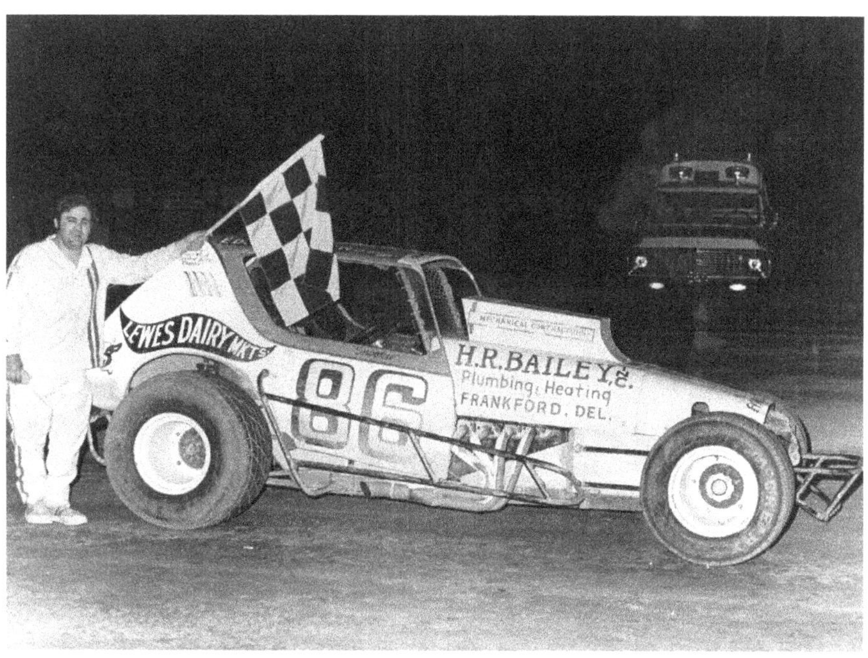

photos from the area, it is easy to see the impact Snookie had on local racing. Almost every car had his shop's name somewhere on it, as Snookie assisted many with sponsorships.

> *When I got into it and had the speed shop, I had two race cars, but two turned into more like thirty-five or forty, because everyone wanted to race and could not afford it. At one point, it almost forced me to quit, but I didn't let it; I did cut back a bit. We were always there for the racers. I would get at the track at two-thirty in the afternoon with our parts truck and I would not get back home until two or three in the morning.*

From selling speed parts to manufacturing Micro Midget chassis and Modified chassis, Snookie always had his hands into racing and has always been the racer's friend.

During those golden years of racing in Delaware, Snookie raced at just about every speedway in Delaware. He now looks back fondly on those days and enjoys all the memories from that period, but one track stands out as his favorite, Little Lincoln. "For five dollars you could have five hundred dollars of fun," says Snookie. One of his best descriptions of the track has been repeated many times and best describes the quarter-mile facility. "For five dollars you could see a fight, you got something decent to eat, you got to see a race, you could fall in love and you could get drunk!" Such were the early, wild days of outlaw racing in Delaware, and pioneers like Snookie led the way for later racers and speed shop owners to follow.

These days, Snookie can still be found along Route 1 in Milton or at an auction, eyeing a rare license plate, of which he has amassed an impressive collection. One thing is for sure, the Delaware racing scene is full of unique and original characters. Snookie is one of those guys you can't help but like, and everyone who knows him has a story about Snookie. He has been one of the steadfast backbones of auto racing in Delaware, and his contributions will long be remembered.

13

BILLY TOWERS

Where U.S. 13 North and South split in Harrington, there once was Towers Gulf Station and Garage. Those stopping by this local landmark could fill up with gas and get their car serviced. And almost always, there was a race car sitting around, waiting for the weekend and the next race. Billy Towers can remember the impression his dad had on him and his love of the automobile and racing in those impressionable first years.

> *My dad was partners with Howard Davis in the late 1950s. Dad would build the motor, and Howard supplied the car. They had drivers like J.R. Jones and Horace Williams. That was back when Georgetown and Wilmington Speedway were operating. Then he started to field cars of his own. Growing up around that had a huge influence on me. I started my driving career in Jalopies at Little Lincoln Speedway. My dad and a lot of other people just could not quite get over the end of the coupe era of racing, but when Doug Morgan went into the woods and scratched out that little speedway in 1967, it was something special. I mean, everyone had a race car. The local junkyards were full of the parts and cars needed for racing at that time. That was really the best time in racing. Anybody that wanted to race a car could afford to run one, whether it be a six cylinder or an eight cylinder. It was such a special time, and this area was so unique. Delaware was just a little bit too far south for the Modified, and it was too far North for the Late Models, so we were kind of in the gray area and really did our own thing.*

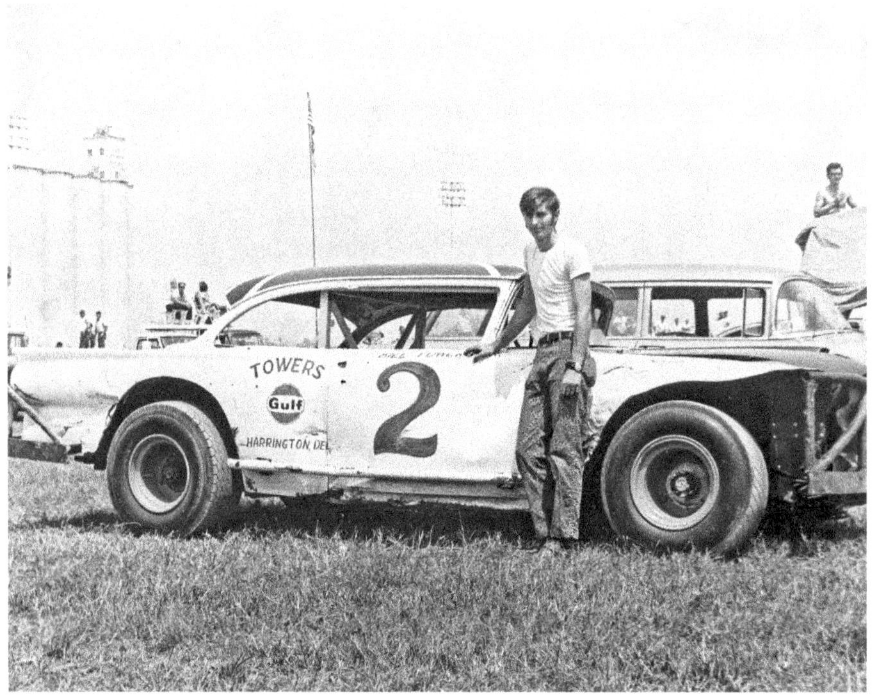

Bill Towers stands next to his race car at the Delaware State Fairgrounds in Harrington, Delaware. *Courtesy of Billy Towers.*

The young Towers sharpened his skills at the small quarter-mile of Little Lincoln, but when asked which speedway was his favorite, the immediate response is Georgetown Speedway. "I have never talked to anyone who raced at Georgetown that said that speedway was not one of their favorites. I always admired Melvin Joseph because he had the ability to know the radius and geometry needed to make a good track. Back then it had a lot more bank than it does now. If you went over the top you were almost guaranteed a good flip."

A love for racing was not the only thing passed down from Billy Tower Sr. to his son. The love for all things Ford was also inherited from his father. Chevrolets tended to be the power plant of choice for most, but not for the Towers. Billy insisted on Ford power in his race cars. "We always pretty much ran Fords. I always paid out of my own pocket in those early days. If it was my car, it had a Ford in it. Now if I was running for someone else, we ran whatever they had in the car." After driving for himself, Towers partnered with owner Ken Covey to drive in the Modified ranks. The partnership was a success, as Towers and Covey won many races in the surrounding area before Towers moved to another local legendary ride, the no. 30 Blue Hen Racing Modified of the Mills Brothers.

> *We made the most of our equipment, for example, when we were racing the no. 21 for Covey, neither Ken or I ever took any money off the table to race. I believed in that and so did Ken, and we made enough money to keep the car going as fast as we could. If we could bring the car home in one piece and finish near the front, we considered that a win.*

While some would credit Towers's success on his driving skill, he was always quick to mention a point often heard in racing. "You are only as good as your equipment. I don't care what everyone says, and yes! I know drivers like Eddie Pettyjohn can really make something happen with an inferior car, but for the most part and your basic racer, you are as only as good as your equipment."

Living in the talent-rich racing town of Milford, Delaware, Towers raced against some of the biggest names in Delaware racing at a time that most consider the golden era of local racing. When asked to name the toughest racer he ever competed against, his quick response is Harold Bunting. "I like Harold, but he would not give you an inch on the track. He would try you every corner on every lap. He applied relentless pressure until he made you choke, and he knew it would happen sooner or later. He was just that good."

While Towers enjoyed the Modifieds, he would end his career in his favorite car, the no. 78 Late Model owned by Raymond White and sponsored by White Construction Company. "I just felt super connected to that car. I could really tell what the car was doing at all times. That car was built by Gerald Chamberland and Guss Greir, so they made it clear that car would only fit a Ford engine in it," Towers jokingly remarks. He would have many victories and success in that car but eventually left racing and refocused his energy and time on his growing and now successful business. When asked about leaving racing and if there are any regrets, Towers simply says: "In racing, if you can't control it, it will control you. I had fun and left at the right time with no regrets. There was more stuff I wanted to do. For a while, I didn't know there was a Saturday night because I was always racing." Making the transition from successful racer to successful businessman, Towers now spends his time operating his business and

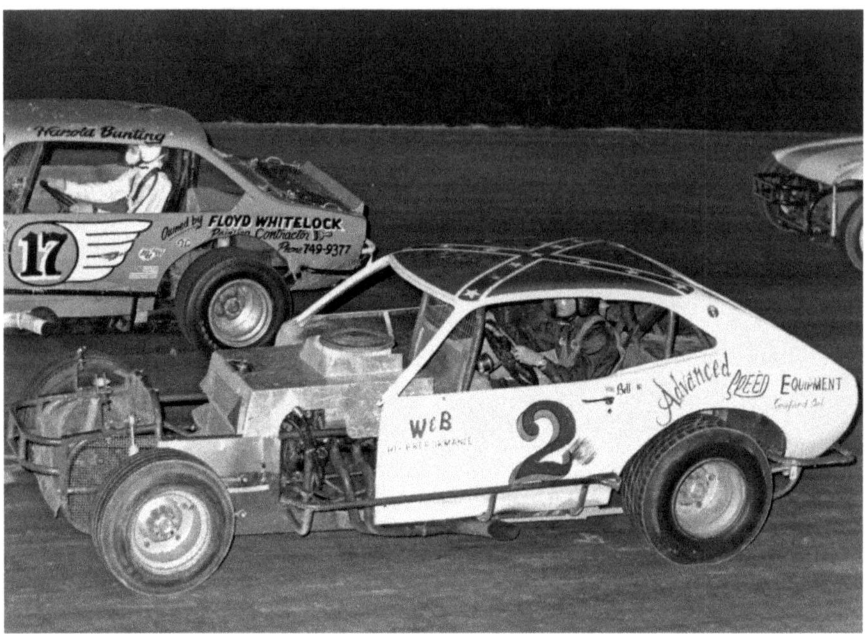

The no. 2 of Billy Towers lines up beside the no. 17 of Harold Bunting at the start of a race. *Courtesy of Billy Towers.*

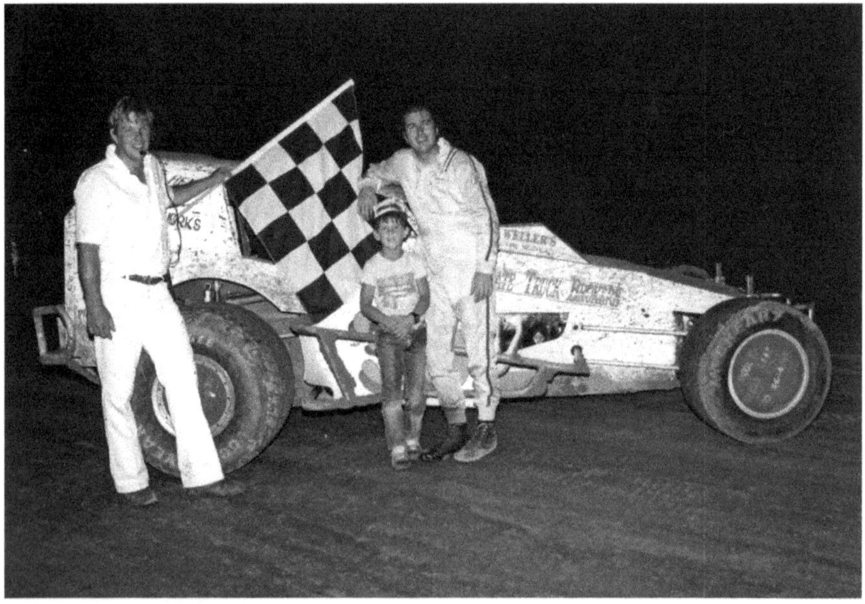

Flagman Bruce Webb congratulates Billy Towers and his son Billy Towers Jr. on another victory. *Courtesy of Billy Towers.*

working on one of his many Fords in his collection of old cars. The Towers' love of cars has been passed down yet again, as Billy's son Bill Towers III is heavily involved in racing both as a driver and a manufacturer of his own Late Model chassis and chassis components in South Carolina. As for Bill, if you see a hot rodded 1930s Ford screaming down the Milford Harrington Highway, give a wave. It's just Billy enjoying life to the fullest and, yes, still driving a Ford!

14

HARRY DUTTON

1932–2016

A true legend of racing, Harry Dutton was one of the most influential personalities in the sport. He had been involved in auto racing since he was a teen and participated in his first race at Harmony Speedway in Maryland. Success on the track would soon follow the young Dutton, as he won the first one-hundred-lap race at Little Lincoln Speedway. Dutton liked the small quarter-mile speedway and went on to win thirteen features in a row at Little Lincoln. He also won multiple championships as well as multiple Driver and Mechanic of the Year awards at the speedway. The popular driver was always recognizable in his no. 88 race car. In an interview conducted in 2014, Dutton explained how he chose his number. "I inherited that number from my brother. He and a few of his buddies used it on a '47 or '48 Ford and did not make out too good with the car. Bobby Reed bought it, and we went from there. The number just came with it. That car just about killed me. I turned that car over just about every week it seemed like. That car gave me a fit."

Dutton's driving career concentrated mostly around US 13 Speedway, Georgetown Speedway and Little Lincoln Speedway in Delaware. Occasionally, he would race outside the state but preferred to race close to his Sussex County home. After hanging up his helmet in 1972, Dutton became a well-known car owner, responsible for giving many racing legends their first shot in a full-size car. Many veterans and top names in racing drove for Dutton as well.

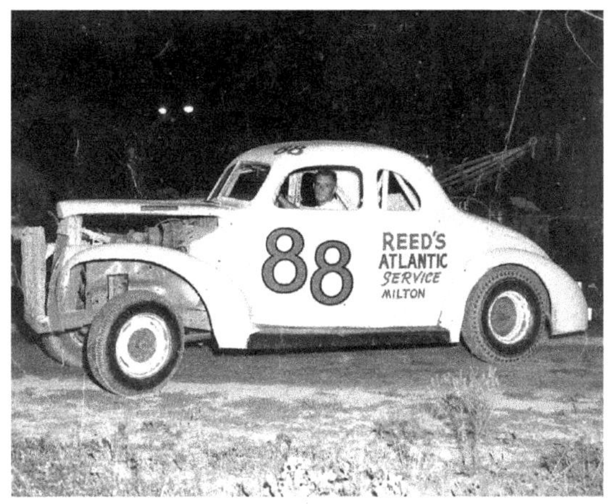

Harry Dutton behind the wheel of one of his early race cars. *Courtesy of Robert Dutton.*

> *When I became an owner, Harold Bunting drove for me at Little Lincoln Speedway after he got out of go-karts. He was working at my repair shop a little bit and helping crew my car. I let Harold eventually run my car when I was asked by Harold Jerman to drive his no. 11 Plymouth. Fred Workman drove for me. Richard Reed drove for me as well in the early days. After I bought a car off of Tom Hagar, he drove for me until another obligation kept him from coming down here to the shore. Lou Johnson finished that year driving for us. The following year, Bobby Wilkins ran for us. Gary Trice, Eddie Pettyjohn, Bob Passwaters, Greg Coverdale and Mel Joseph Jr. all spent time driving for us at some point.*

Dutton was never too far away from something with a wheel. He made a living owning an automobile shop and trucking company and transferred the skills used in those businesses directly to racing. He was known for his ability to build potent big block motors that could run with many of the top engine manufacturers of the time. Harry Dutton's son Robert talks about his dad's mechanical prowess and how he started racing under the watchful eye of his father.

> *He made good power in his motors. He was one of the last guys that could completely build everything on a race car from the ground up. Even back during his Little Lincoln days, he built his own motors. I remember getting started racing with Dad. We had an old Weld chassis sitting back in the weeds covered up with honeysuckle. I grew up watching him as a car owner and watching everyone race for him. So, when I got old enough, I told him, "Hey, I want to race." He said, "Well, there is the car back in the weeds*

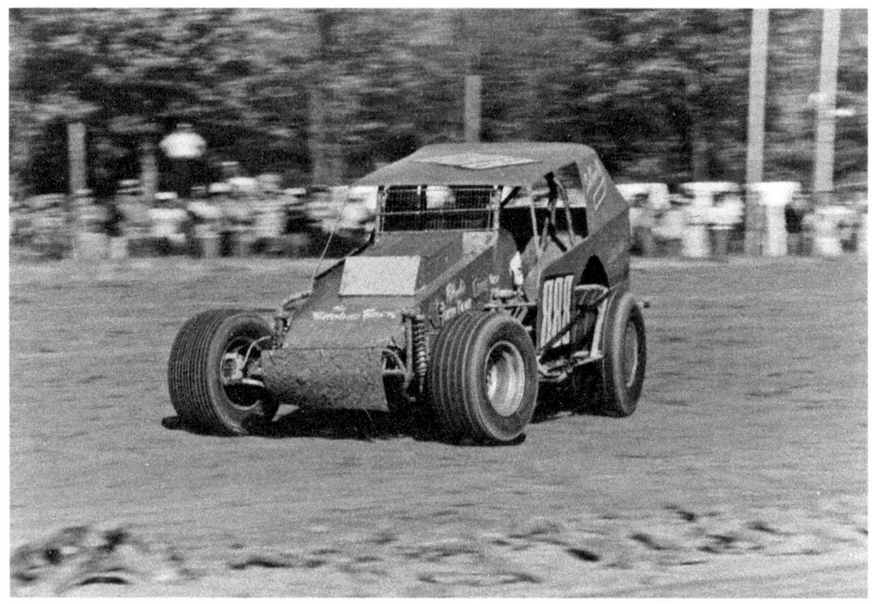

Pictured in his rookie season, Robert Dutton carries on the Dutton family racing legacy. *Courtesy of Don and Linda Allen, D&L Photos.*

> *over there, go get her." So, me and a buddy of mine went and pulled the car out of the weeds and cleaned it up and moved it into the shop. I had a 1982 Chevy Camaro at that time. I asked Dad what was it going to take to put this race car back together. He called Snookie and got prices on a steering box and prices on some motor parts. He told me it was going to take sixteen hundred dollars to get the race car going. I had my Camaro, and my sister wanted it something bad. So I called her up and said, "If you want this Camaro, I will take sixteen hundred dollars for it." So, she bought it and brought the money down that day. When she handed me the money, I handed it right back to her and told her to take it to Snookie for the parts, because I did not have a car to drive on the road anymore. Not long after that, I took that car to Harrington to race.*

Robert Dutton continues to carry on the family racing traditions passed down from his father. On any Saturday night, you will find him behind the wheel of his no. 888 Modified powered by an engine he built himself using lessons learned from his father. Harry Dutton will long be remembered not only as an excellent driver, mechanic and owner, but also for being an honest, straight-shooting racer who told you like it was.

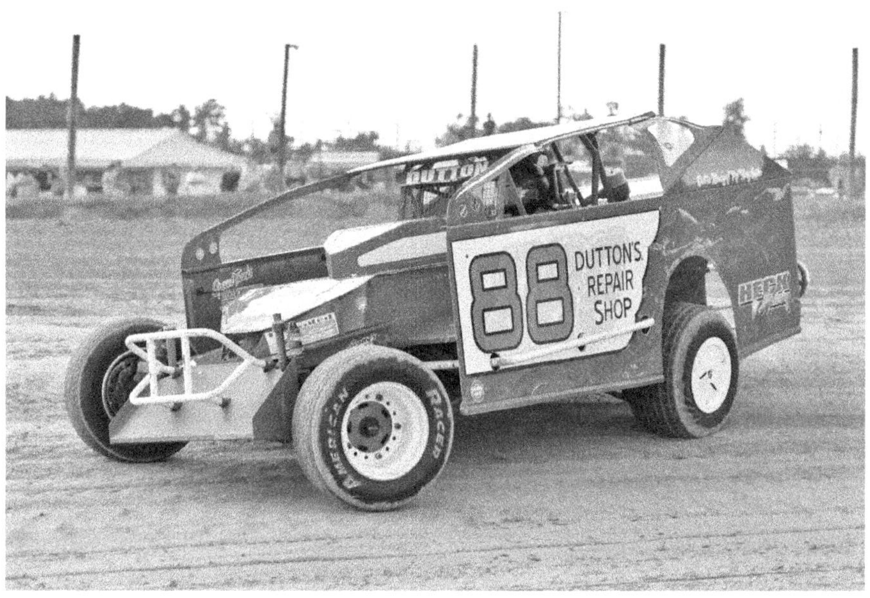

Siding through the corner, driver Robert Dutton pilots his Modified, painted to commemorate and honor his dad's early race cars. *Courtesy of Landstone Photography.*

"When Dad told you something, that was the way it was going to be. He was really old school. If you told him you were going to come by the shop Wednesday, he fully expected you to be there. He was very much a man of his word and expected the same out of others. Dad played hard and worked hard. He lived life to the fullest, and he lived it on his terms, whether you liked it or you didn't."

We should all be so lucky and blessed to live life on our terms like Harry Dutton did. A prime example of hard work and dedication to one's craft, Harry Dutton's legend will live on as an example for all to follow.

15

EUGENE MILLS

Eugene Mills and the family's no. 30 Modified have become historic fixtures in racing, not only in Delaware, but also up and down the East Coast. Mills's career as a driver and owner have led him from his humble beginnings at Little Lincoln Speedway all the way to his induction into the hallowed grounds of the Northeast Dirt Modified Hall of Fame, the only person from Delaware ever to be inducted. Mills received his love of racing and the no. 30 from his father, also named Eugene. He explains those early days of racing, how the family ended up with the number 30 and how he went from being a driver to becoming an owner.

I got my love of racing from my father. He had a car that we raced at Georgetown Speedway right after Melvin Joseph built it. The speedway was NASCAR sanctioned at the time, and the car number came from NASCAR. It was assigned to us, and we have used it ever since. They eventually got out of the sport, but as soon as I could, I bought a race car and ran Little Lincoln Speedway with it in the Hobby class. I won the first race out in that car. I eventually moved up a division and started racing at Georgetown and Delaware International Speedway (formerly US 13 Speedway). I had a good time driving! That all came to an end one night at US 13 Speedway. I was running in the Sportsman class at the time, and it was the first night US 13 expanded their track to a half-mile oval. I crossed the finish line in second or third place, and at that time they ran the Hobby class with the Sportsman class at the same time. I had a car in

> *front of me going way slower. I swerved to avoid it and ended up hitting a ditch they had in the infield, wrecking and breaking my back. I eventually recovered, but that was the end of my driving days. I owned Sportsman cars for a few years before jumping up to the Big Block Modified division, where we have raced ever since.*

Mills formed the Blue Hen Racing Team in 1977 with a few friends and brother Paul Mills. It was the beginning of one of the most successful Modified teams of all time. While no official number exists, it has been estimated that Mills's win total as an owner is somewhere between six hundred and seven hundred victories. The list of drivers who have sat behind the wheel of the no. 30 is indeed impressive. Mills's top-notch ride attracted some of the biggest names in the sport. Drivers like Fred Workman, Haines Tull, John Kozak, Harold Bunting, Bill Towers, Bobby Wilkins, Gary Gollub, Kenny Brightbill, Bob McCreadie, Dave Kelly, Jack Johnson, HJ Bunting, Jamie Mills, Jordan Watson and Joseph Watson have all taken turns piloting no. 30 cars owned by Mills. Perhaps one of the most memorable wins for Mills came in 1988 at Super Dirt Week at Syracuse, New York. The 1988 Syracuse Miller High Life 300 was easily the "Super Bowl" of Modified racing at the

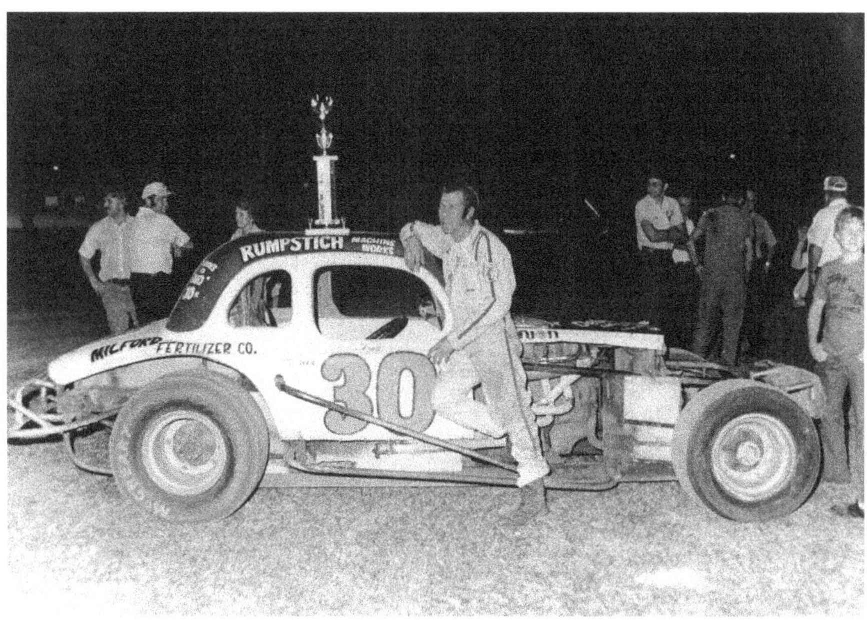

Fred Workman shows off his first-place trophy after the no. 30 Modified raced to Victory Lane for owner Eugene Mills. *Courtesy of the Workman family.*

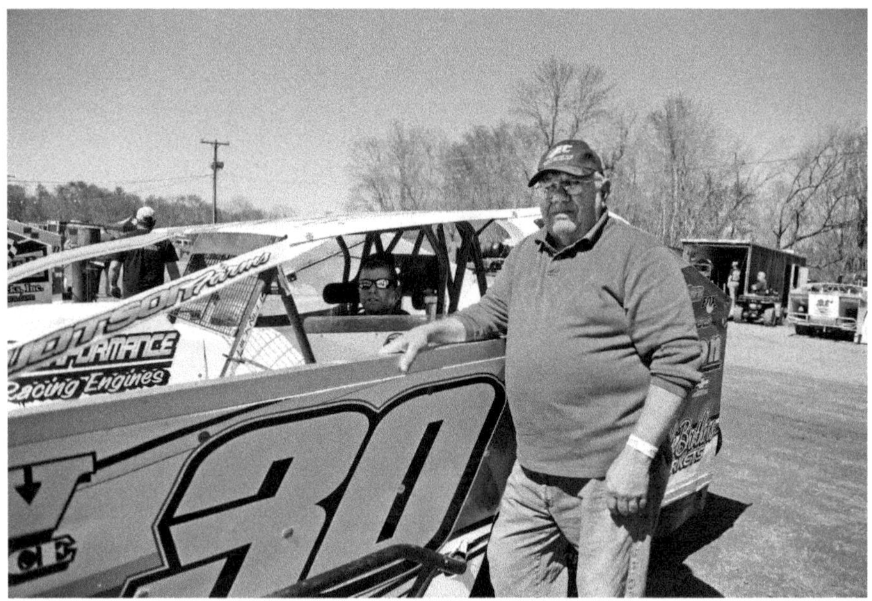

Car owner and Dirt Motorsports Hall of Famer Eugene Mills stands next to his Modified, with son Jamie Mills ready to take to the track. *Courtesy of Rick Sweeten Images.*

time. The Moody Mile, a one-mile oval at the New York State Fairgrounds, tested drivers and their machines to the limit. A win there secured your name in the history books. Mills remembers the preparations for that race and what would be one of his biggest wins of his career as a car owner.

> *That was a good win. That was the last time that race was won with a homebuilt car. Kenny Brightbill built that chassis. He drew it out on the garage floor how he wanted to build it. We had a brand-new Olsen car at the shop, and about three weeks before the big race at Syracuse, he came to me and said, "We can't win the race with that car. If you want to win that race, let me build a car the way I want and I will win the race." So we all went to work on it, and the result speaks for itself.*

To this day, Eugene Mills is the only Delaware owner to win Super Dirt Week. While the team had many other big wins up and down the coast, there is one race that remains Mills's favorite and most sentimental win: the Camp Barnes Race. It is held annually in Delaware to benefit the Delaware State Police camp for children called Camp Barnes. Eugene explains his special connection to the race.

> *Out of all of the races we have won, and that is a lot of races, the Camp Barnes races stand above all the rest. We have won that race multiple times. The Delaware State Police and what they do through Camp Barnes has got to be one of my favorite organizations. My father was in the Sheriff's Department before he passed, and he really supported Camp Barnes, and I guess it has just been passed down to me. When my son, Jamie Mills, won it for the first time, it was just a great feeling. I won the Sportsman race at Camp Barnes back in the 1950s, when the race was originally held at Georgetown Speedway. It is just a really special race for us locals around here.*

Eugene Mills counts his victories and championships with his son Jamie among his most special. Recently retired from racing, Jamie has had a legendary career driving his father's no. 30 Modified car. Winning many championships and major races along the way, Jamie will long be remembered as one of the most entertaining and exciting drivers to come out of the state of Delaware. With Jamie's retirement, one might expect Eugene to walk away from racing after more than fifty years in the sport.

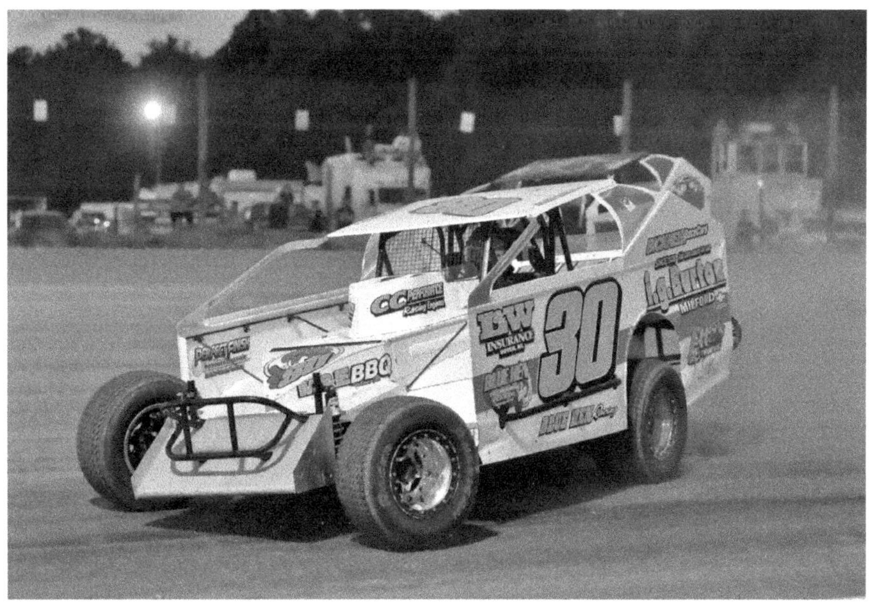

Jamie Mills pilots the no. 30 Modified owned by his father, Eugene, during his final year of competition at Delaware International Speedway. *Courtesy of Landstone Photography.*

Such is not the case. His passion is as great now as when he started. He looks forward to the future and will continue to field a no. 30 Modified race car, with grandson Joseph Watson taking over driving duties. According to Eugene Mills, he does not plan on walking away anytime soon.

> *I don't see an end in sight. As long as I keep enjoying what I am doing, I am going to keep fielding a car. I love racing and I love the people that are involved in racing. I do really miss the days of old when you could be creative and build a lot of the cars yourself. It is a different game now, but I still enjoy the sport as much as I ever have. All my grandsons are involved in racing in some way. My one grandson, Jeremy Harrington, is working for a NASCAR team down in North Carolina, and my other two grandsons, Joseph and Jordan, are racing Modifieds. After all these years, I still enjoy racing and everything that goes with it.*

16

KEN COVEY

For every great driver, often behind the scenes there is a great mechanic and car owner. For many years, Ken Covey fielded some of the cleanest, sharpest and most competitive race cars out of his Covey's Car Care business in Seaford, Delaware. Driven by some of the area's best drivers, such as Stan Busby, Haines Tull, Bill Towers, Gary Gollub and Ken's son Mike Covey, Ken's cars were a threat to win whenever they showed up to a track. After graduating high school in 1959 and working on the family farm, Covey served in the U.S. Navy and knew upon his return home that he did not want to spend his days behind a plow or milking cows. Covey explains how he found his passion in the garage business:

> *In the navy, I was a machinist mate and gained a lot of knowledge about all things mechanical. When I returned home, I went to work for Tri-State Engineering in Salisbury, Maryland, doing refrigeration, air-conditioning and boiler work. After a few years, I decided I wanted to work for myself and have my own commercial refrigeration business. I did not have any money, so I opened a gas station, because I knew I could do all the work associated with owning one. I thought when I get enough money, I will get out of the gas station and repair business and open my own air-conditioning business. Well, that never happened. I still used my air-conditioning experience to install air conditioners in cars during the '60s and thought that by putting air conditioners in cars I would be able to get in the air-conditioner business quicker, but the more you get invested in what you are already doing, the harder it was to get out.*

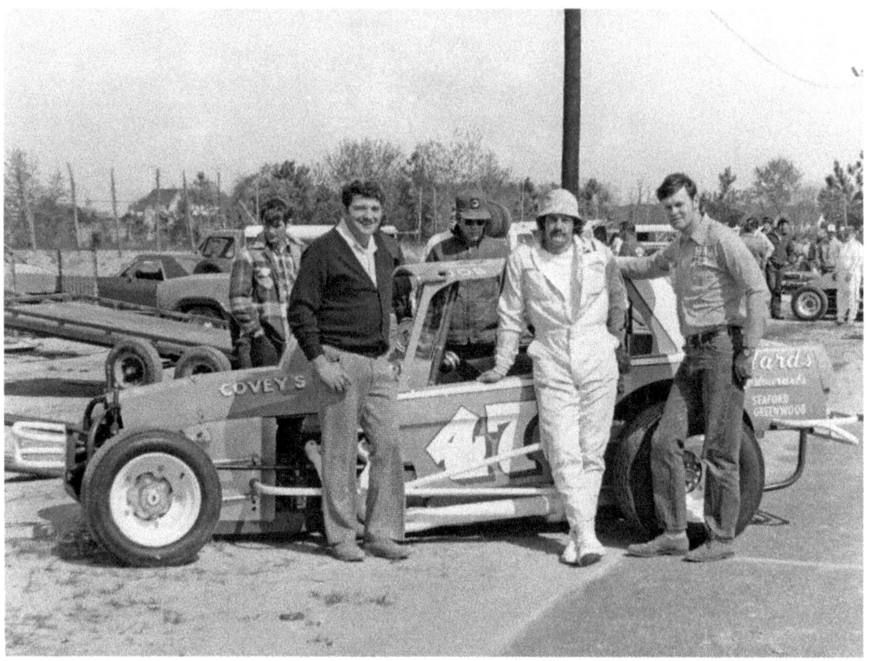

From left to right are car sponsor Aubrey Dillard, driver Stan Busby and car owner Ken Covey at Georgetown Speedway. *Courtesy of Ken Covey.*

Operating his own garage since 1965, Covey always had a keen interest in racing and shared that interest with racing friends Norris "Speedy" Reed and Walt Breeding. In 1973, Ken and Walt started assembling and building Tobias-based cars on the side at night.

With over seventy-five feature wins—forty to forty-five of those with driver Gary Gollub—Covey still says his biggest win was the very first one. He continued a winning tradition throughout his career and, in his most successful year as an owner, collected fourteen wins. Covey remembers one of his favorite wins, the GT100 sponsored by Kendal Motor Oil at Georgetown Speedway:

> *That was one of the first races that had a sponsor that put some money out there for us to win. We were not used to running races of that length, and Towel City Recap tires at that time were a real hot deal. We also had what we called Firestone Diamond tires. So, I took a chance and decided to run these new Firestone tires in the one-hundred-lap race. We knew we were going to have to change tires during the race, so the crew practiced pit*

stops just like you see the NASCAR teams do on Sunday. We had it down to where if there was a caution, we could change the tire and get back on the speedway without losing a lap. The whole change took about thirty seconds. When the race got going with our driver Stan Busby, I would stand on the corner and watch the car during the cautions. As the car rolled by slowly, I would look at the tire to see if the tread was holding up. So, I just kept signaling Stan to keep out on the track and not come in. Well, we never came in once for tires and we never relinquished the lead during that race. There were a whole lot of upset people because no one thought they could go 100 laps. They thought we pulled a fast one, but those were the same tires anyone could buy that day. No one thought they would last the entire race. That was when racing was real fun and you kind of invented your own mousetrap type of deal. A lot of people didn't know any more than we did. It was just a guessing game sometimes.

Legendary driver Gary Gollub fondly remembers his time driving the no. 21 Modified for Covey. "Ken was a great car owner, he got everything out of the money he spent through good planning and maintenance! I know we

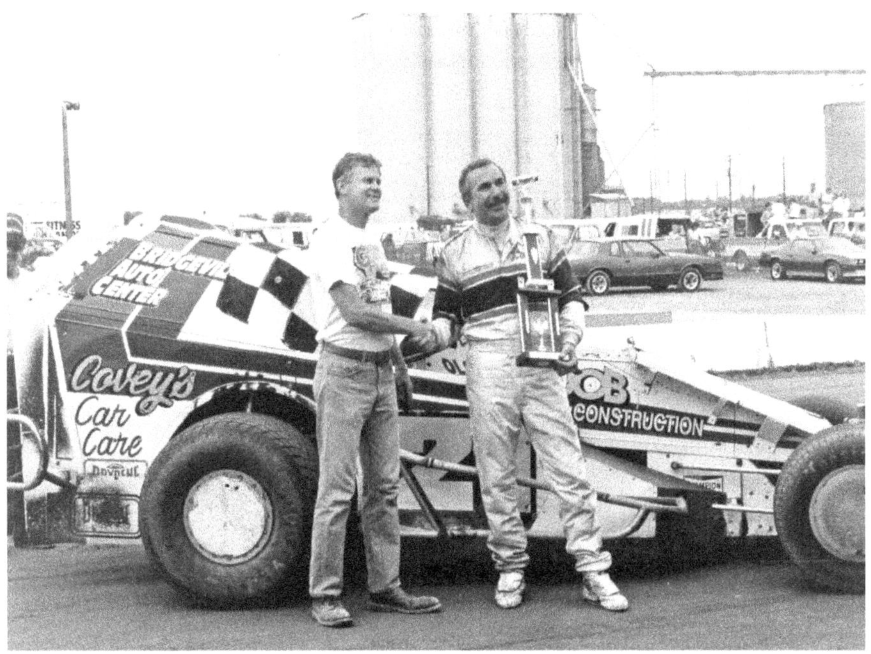

Owner Ken Covey congratulates his winning driver, Gary Gollub, at the Delaware State Fairgrounds in Harrington, Delaware. *Courtesy of Ken Covey.*

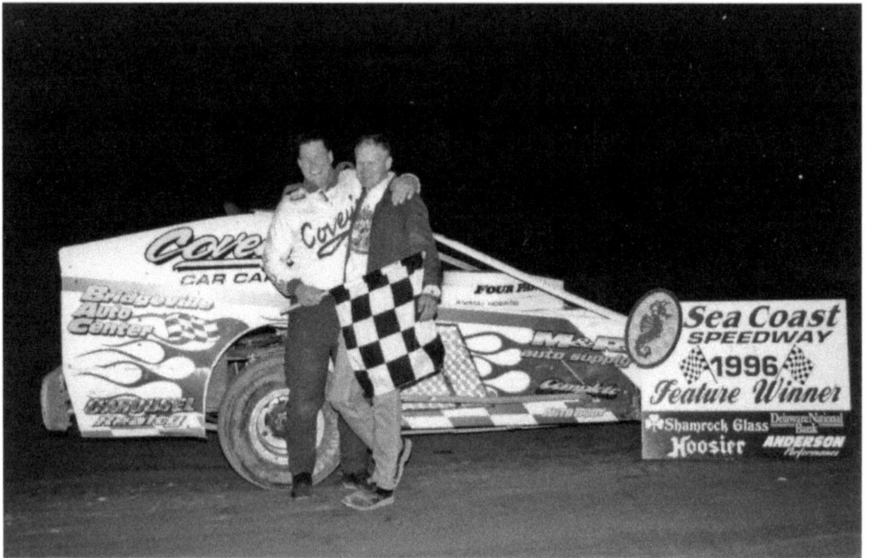

Driver Mike Covey and his dad, Ken Covey, celebrate another victory at Georgetown Speedway, then named Sea Coast Speedway, in 1996. *Courtesy of Ken Covey.*

beat a lot of teams that spent a lot more money. Ken was one of the best car owners I drove for. He and Robert Reed [crew chief] really worked well with getting the car to my liking. I really miss those good old days!"

Through feature wins and championships, Ken Covey will long be remembered as a racer, competitor and gentleman. Bring up Ken's name, and anyone who has been around racing will be quick to tell you how great a guy he is. Ken tells one last story that really shows the respect racers had for him.

> *In the earlier years, we had the Delmarva Auto Racing Association. George Reed was the president of the club and there were a bunch of us who helped with the club at that time. George moved away, and Donald Joseph took over as president, and I became vice-president. We all did our part. One night at Georgetown Bobby Wilkins won the race and Lester Nailor was in the race as well. I can't remember what happened exactly on the track between the two, but Lester parked in front of Bobby's car to keep him from getting the accolades from winning. They came to hook up the wrecker to Lester's car because he was not supposed to be there and kept interrupting things, but every time they tried to hook it up, he kept moving the car and this went on for some time before it came to an end. So, the association made*

the decision that Lester would have to be suspended a couple of weeks for his actions. Donald was the president and was resigning his position and said there was no way he was going to go talk to him, so that left me to do it. I thought, "Well, if it's gotta be done, it's gotta be done." I had known Lester before, and he seemed like an OK guy, but when he put his helmet on he was competitive. I walked up to Lester and put my arm around him, and he said to me, "Is there something you got to tell me?" I said, "Yep, you have a couple of weeks off." He just turned to me and said, "OK." It was not a problem at all!

There are many more stories like this involving Ken Covey, and they are a true testament to the respect and admiration all have for him after many years of running one of Delaware's most competitive and successful race teams.

17

RON SLADE

Perhaps one of the most inspiring racers to ever suit up and drive a race car in Delaware was Ron Slade. Slade served his country in the army as a rifle platoon leader in the Tropic Lightning Twenty-Fifth Division. During his service in the Vietnam War, Slade lost both of his legs. The thought of driving a race car with this challenge may have been too much for most, but not for Slade, who never let his challenges get in the way of his dreams. His dedication to country and his positive attitude despite challenging circumstances made him a fan favorite wherever he ran. Slade remembers those early times racing in Delaware.

> *My plan was to race motorcycles when I got back from the war because I did a little bit of racing before I went to Vietnam. I was still in and out of Walter Reed Hospital for almost two years with my injuries from the war. That's when I started competing in the Six-Cylinder class at US 13 Speedway. I didn't even have my legs yet! I Ace bandaged a two-by-four to myself and drove with that. I still used the stock location for the brake and gas pedal, but I just made them a little bigger than normal. I drove a dump truck for Charlie West, who was right across from US 13 Speedway. When I first got married, we had a trailer not too far away from the speedway, so it makes sense that I started my racing career at US 13 Speedway. I went to Georgetown and Little Lincoln to race as well. I always wanted to race. My first car came from Junior West. It was a six-cylinder, and we renumbered it and did a little bit of work to it and went*

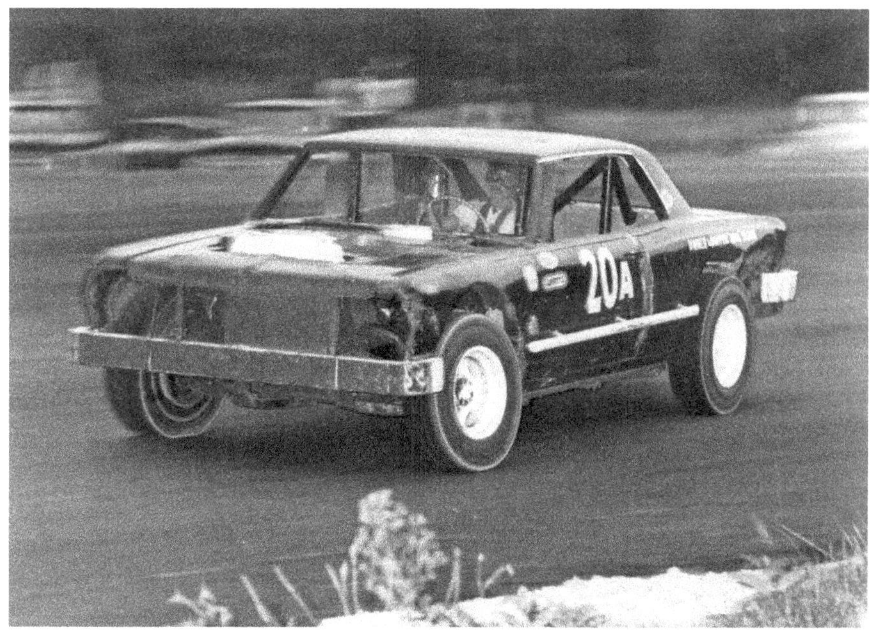

Ron Slade sliding the no. 20A through the turn at speed. *Courtesy of Keith Short.*

> *racing. After that first car, I built my own race cars from then on. I wanted my number to be 20, but when I showed up to the track, someone already had that number, so we just added an A behind the number. So, my number was always the 20A after that.*

Slade's determination, service and drive made quite an impression on many people. If you look at the early Camp Barnes patches that were so popular with fans and handed out at the annual Camp Barnes Race, you will notice the car used on the patch bears the no. 20A in honor of Ron Slade. Slade remembers those days fondly. "I remember Bodie Bodenhiser really well when I ran the Six-Cylinder class. He was one of the toughest competitors. That car of his would absolutely fly, and he was a good driver. He was always fast. Sonny Brittingham, Don Twilly and Walt Breeding were names I remember well also from those days."

Slade would eventually move to Pennsylvania, carrying his love for racing with him. After starting in the Six-Cylinder division on the tracks at Delaware, Slade would progress into racing in the Modified and Sprint Car divisions at some of the area's toughest tracks, like Bridgeport Speedway, Reading Fairgrounds, Selinsgrove Speedway and Williams Grove Speedway.

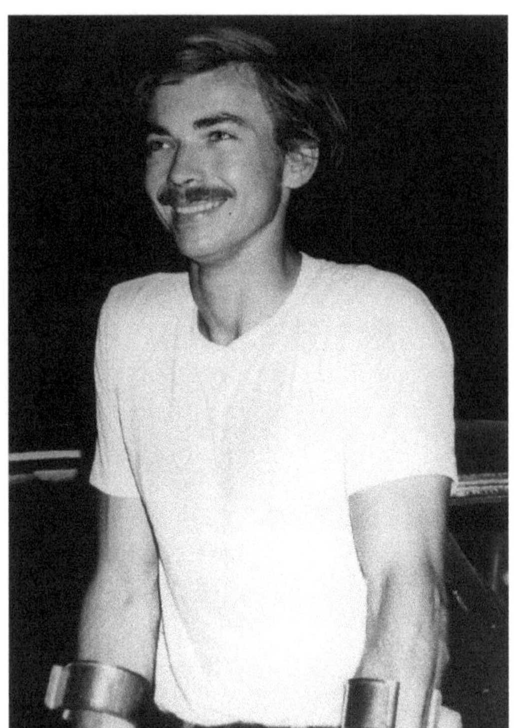

Right: Vietnam veteran and American hero Ron Slade stood tall against the competition and inspired many. *Courtesy of Keith Short*.

Below: Ron Slade in Victory Lane after winning a feature event. *Courtesy of Keith Short*.

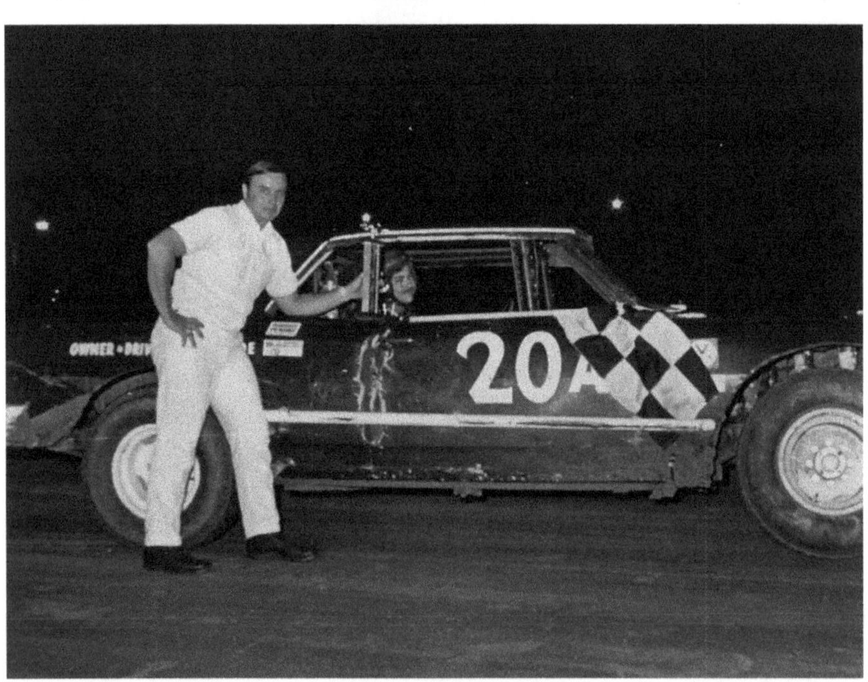

I started racing when you made your own cars and built them yourself in Delaware. By the time I was racing at Reading in a Modified, things really had started to change. I didn't have a clue what I was doing, because those guys up there were so knowledgeable about setting the cars up. I was kind of lost at first, but once we figured it out, we had some good runs. I switched to Sprint Cars and finally stopped racing because of the rising cost to race every week.

Slade would eventually move his family to the West Coast and settle down in Southern California, a place he had visited while in the service.

I love it out here, it is beautiful. We moved to California in 1987. I had a welding, fabricating and machine shop. I continued to race when I moved out here. I did some desert racing and motocross racing on quads and motorcycles. We ran a buggy in some of the desert races as well. I still enjoy riding them, although I no longer race. I enjoy riding mountain bikes with my son now and try to stay as active as I can.

Now seventy-eight years old, Slade still sets an example for all to follow. On any day, you can find him hiking the mountains or taking a ride on his mountain bike with family, living every moment to the fullest with no excuses and no limits. His racing history makes him a legend of Delaware auto racing, but his service to country and zest for life make him a true example of how we all should be thankful for what we have and live each moment to the fullest.

18

DAVID HILL

One of racing's great families, the Hill family has been at the forefront of Late Model racing in Delaware since the early 1970s. David Hill, the all-time Late Model win leader at Delaware International Speedway with 140 wins and five track championships, remembers how his family got their start in racing.

> *The person who really got my family started in racing was Bob Walls Jr. from over in Ridgely, Maryland. My dad, Larry Hill, knew the Walls through our business, Hill's Electric, and we started going to watch him race. Then, in 1973, my dad bought a car from Bob Walls. It was a six-cylinder Falcon bodied Sportsman car, and Bob Walls drove it for us. At first, my dad did not tell my mom it was his car. He told her it was owned by a friend of his. In 1974, we changed it around a bit and put a Maverick body on it and raced it. After sitting out in 1975, we came back in 1976 with a Late Model and my dad took over the driving duties. Dad drove the car in 1976, 1977 and 1978. In 1976, the car was a 1967 Chevelle, and then in 1977, he debuted the 1967 Camaro. In 1978, I made my debut in the mini stock class as I got my first start in a four-cylinder Pinto.*

From the beginning, it was always a family affair for the Hills. With patriarch Larry Hill jumping into racing, it was not long before both his sons, David and Steve, would follow in their father's footsteps. Racing as a team, Steve carried the number 10 on the side of his Late Model while David ran the

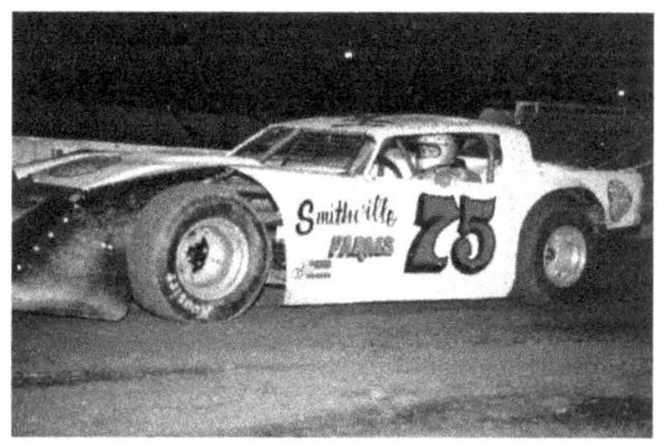

David Hill lines up for a feature event in one of his early Late Model race cars. *Courtesy of the Hill family.*

more familiar no. 75 along the side of his red Late Model race car. The color red and no. 75 would become synonymous with the Hill family. David Hill recounts the story of how the family came to run the number for such a long time.

> *The first car we bought from Bob Walls was no. 22, so to make it easy we renumbered the car no. 222. It looked like his car, but it was not the same number. Jack Abbott, a friend of my dad who helped me all through my racing career, for some reason always called that car "old six bits," so the next year when we changed the car to the Maverick body, we decided to change the color of the car from the orange that Bob Walls ran to red, which has always been our family's favorite color. At the same time, Dad decided that in pesos, six bits equaled 75, so that is how he came up with the number 75 for the car. Since Dad put that number on the car, we ran it until I retired from racing in 2013.*

To say the Hill family found success during their tenure in racing would be an understatement. Larry Hill won 20 feature events and 2 Delaware International Speedway Points Championships during his brief racing career. Brother Steve collected 8 feature wins during his Late Model racing career. Along with having the most longevity of the Hill family in racing, David's résumé is also most impressive and puts him up there with the all-time greats of racing. At Delaware International Speedway alone, he has won over 140 features, landing him on top of the all-time feature win list at the speedway for the Late Model division. David's consistency at Delaware International also netted 5 track championships during his long career. While spending most of his career focusing on racing at Delaware International Speedway, David Hill also ventured to other tracks, enough to record 9 wins at Potomac Speedway, 35 wins and one track championship at Georgetown Speedway and 1 win at the famous Late Model mecca, Hagerstown Speedway. Racing for over thirty-five years, Hill remembers some of his favorite wins.

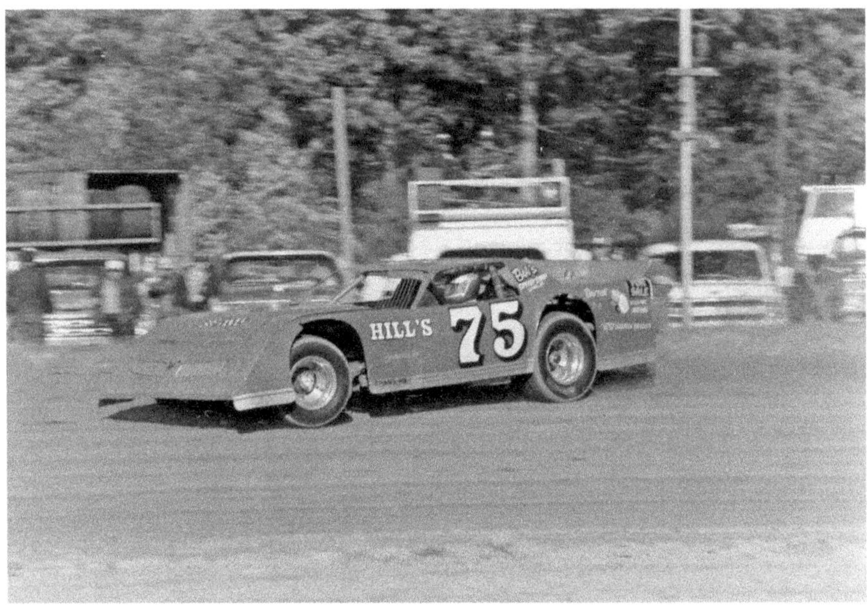

David Hill finished out his career as the all-time Late Model win leader at Delaware International Speedway. *Courtesy of Don and Linda Allen, D&L Photos.*

> *They are all special, but that first year-end Delaware State Championship race we won, which was in 1986, was really special. We had a brand-new Bullit Chassis car, and it was the first race with it. At that point in time, Eddie Pettyjohn was so dominant and had been winning a bunch of races. We were able to beat him and Ray Kable that day, so it was nice to finally beat the best at one of the biggest races of the year. That was a big win for us. My other favorite win was at Hagerstown Speedway. That was just such a hard place to win in a Late Model in the '80s and '90s, because the best Late Model drivers around raced there every week. It was a tricky track, and you had to just be so smooth and so exact to be a winner there.*

Looking back on his career and the success the family has had, Hill, who retired from driving in 2013, reflects on the important part to winning races.

> *I would really like people to know this about our racing team. Even though I always got the credit for winning the races and championship, it was really a team effort. I could not have done any of it without my parents backing, but also all the guys who backed me over the years and were on*

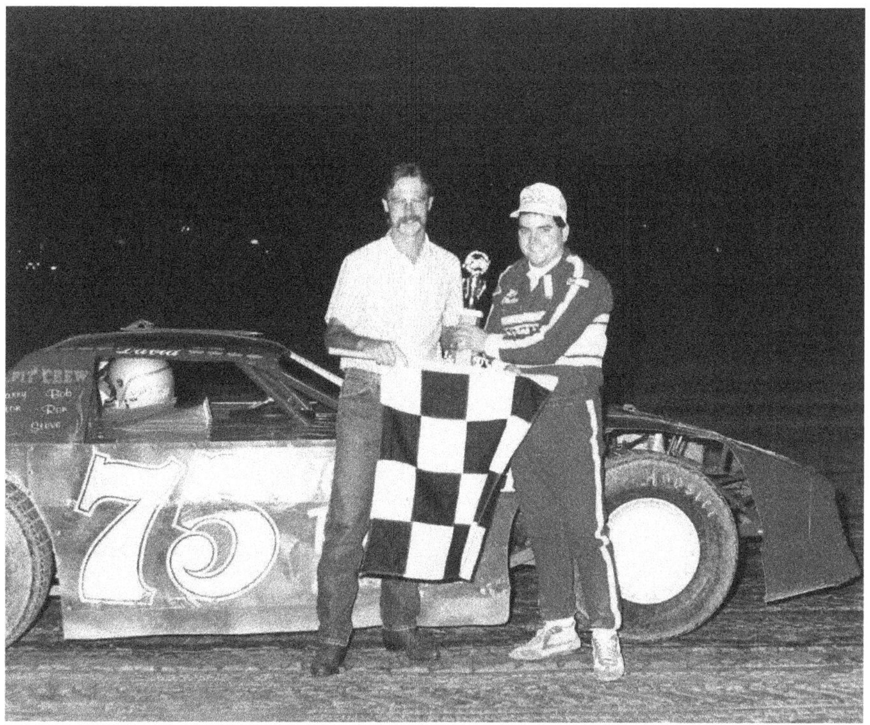

David Hill (*left*) receives his trophy for the night's victory from fellow racing legend Bobby Wilkins. *Courtesy of the Hill family.*

> *the pit crews, my wife and everyone. It took all of us to win. I was just the lucky guy who got to sit in the car and drive it. The preparation and the hard work and sacrifice back in the shop is what made us winners. It was just not always about what happened on the track.*

Some of the nicest, classiest people you will ever know, the Hill family still operates its family business and continues to love racing. Many fans still hold fond memories of the always clean and spotless red no. 75 running around the track on its way to another victory. If you were privileged enough to watch them race, it's a sight that is seared into your memory!

19

TOM GARN

1926–1984

One of the little-known facts about racing in Delaware is that NASCAR driver and team owner Richard Childress got his start right here in the First State from a gentleman named Tom Garn. Who knew that a little team based in Seaford, Delaware, would evolve into one of NASCAR's most legendary powerhouse teams. Tom Garn probably did not have a clue how much of an influence he would have on racing when he bought his first race car back in 1968. His son and local racer Bill Garn remembers his dad's humble start.

> *We were living in Akron, Ohio, at the time. In 1968, Dad bought a 1966 Chevelle from the insurance company. He had a cousin at the time who was running some local asphalt tracks in Ohio, and Dad would help him out every now and then by buying him a case of oil for his car. Dad finally decided he was going to have his own car, and he built that 1966 Chevelle in a garage in a pretty nice neighborhood for the time, which I am pretty sure the neighbors were not too happy about. Once we got it together, he had Chuck Wright build an engine for it and we went racing. Dad never drove the car; he was always an owner.*

Eventually making his way to Delaware, Tom Garn put his roots down in Seaford. As part owner of L.C. Newton Trucking Company, Garn quickly continued his passion for racing and bought a Camaro to run on asphalt in the NASCAR Grand National East series. Tom Garn's brother Nick

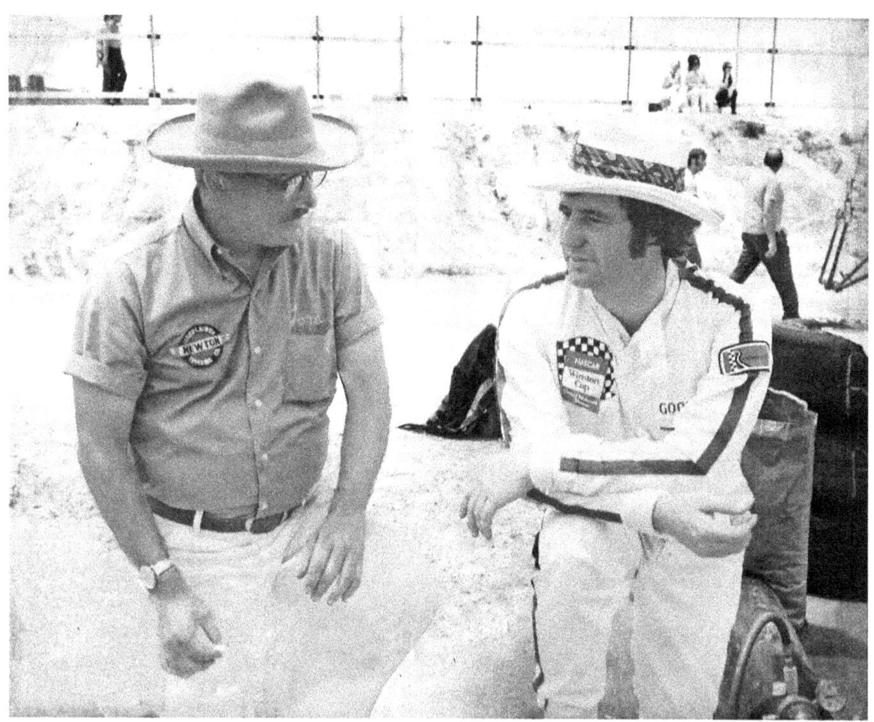

Car owner Tom Garn (*left*) and driver Richard Childress (*right*) have a discussion before the start of a NASCAR race at Dover International Speedway. *Courtesy of Bill Garn.*

helped greatly with the mechanics of all their cars, and Tommy Lechlider of Seaford drove it for a little bit as the no. 61 before Garn's path crossed with Richard Childress. Future driver Richard Childress remembers how he met Tom and how they got involved together in racing.

> *We were running in the Grand National East Series back in 1972. We were at Islip Speedway in New York, and Tom's driver had a problem and could not race, so Tom asked me if I would drive the car for him. I had my own car that night, so I let my brother, Ronnie, start the race in my car so that we would get the starting money, while I drove Tom's car. I finished pretty well that night in Tom's car. I think maybe second or third out of the non-Cup drivers who were in the race, because the race was really a mix between Cup and non-Cup drivers. Tom was impressed with what I did with the car. That is really how I got my start with Tom Garn. At the end of that year, Tom said, "I want to build a Cup car, and I want you to drive for me." In 1973, we went to Daytona. We had a Bobby Allison*

> *chassis in the car and went out and qualified well. We ran pretty well in the race, and we ended up racing for him all year long. In 1974, Tom decided that he wanted to get out of the sport, so he sold me the race team, the truck and trailer, everything. I borrowed some money from NASCAR, and he financed some of the money. Tom Garn played a tremendous role in Richard Childress Racing. He played a role in my success as a driver and in building my way as an owner. I became an owner and driver in 1974 because of Tom Garn.*

Even after Childress bought the team, Garn and his L.C. Newton Trucking Company stayed on as the primary sponsor for years. When Garn owned the team, they ran no. 96. Once ownership changed, Childress switched to the famous no. 3, which would become affiliated with his team until today. The opportunity that Garn gave Childress set him on a path to become one of the most prolific owners in NASCAR history. Since buying the team from Garn, Childress has amassed over two hundred wins in his career as a car owner. Along the way, he has collected over thirteen driver's championships, including six in NASCAR's Premier Cup series with NASCAR Hall of Fame driver, the late Dale Earnhardt. Not bad for

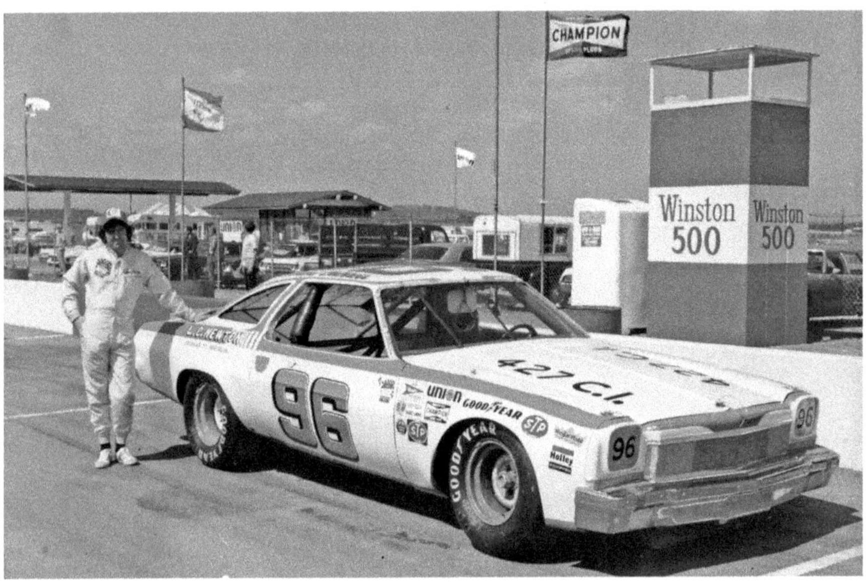

Driver Richard Childress stands next to the no. 96 L.C. Newton Trucking Company race car owned by Tom Garn of Seaford, Delaware. *Courtesy of Bill Garn.*

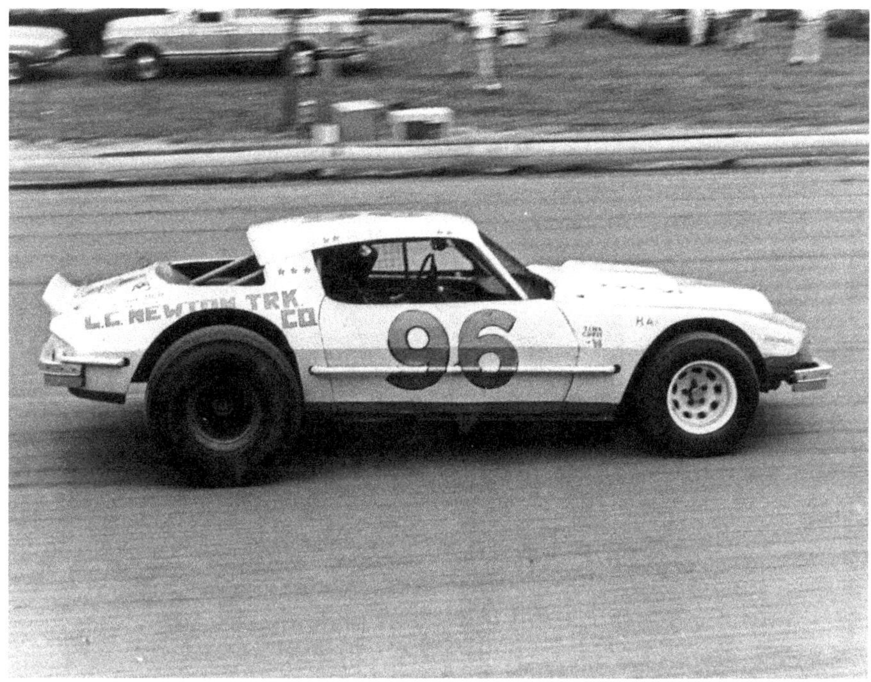

Bill Garn in his feature-winning Late Model sponsored by his father's L.C. Newton Trucking Company. *Courtesy of Bill Garn.*

a team that started in a garage in the small town of Seaford, Delaware. Today, Richard Childress Racing continues to field cars in NASCAR Premier Series, winning the 2018 Daytona 500 with grandson Austin Dillon driving. Richard Childress has never forgotten the influence and kindness Garn showed him during those early years, and he comments on Garn's role in not only in racing in Delaware but also in helping Richard Childress Racing get started in NASCAR.

> *Tom Garn was huge in racing in Seaford, Delaware. Tom was very passionate about racing. He ran some dirt race cars up there. He didn't drive himself, but he owned the cars. He played a huge role in racing in Delaware, as far as the success of racing up there. Tom played a major role in getting Richard Childress Racing get started. If it hadn't been for Tom selling me the race team in 1974 and helping me finance it, I probably would not be here today.*

Passion and excellence are traits that all successful people share. From a humble garage in Seaford to the state-of-the-art Richard Childress Racing team shop in Welcome, North Carolina, Richard Childress has come a long way. Front and center in his museum is one of his first race cars, sponsored by L.C. Newton Trucking Company and owned by Garn. Always racing Chevrolets throughout his career, Tom Garn's legacy lives on every time Richard Childress Racing hits the track.

20
WALT MESSICK
1918–1992

Walter Messick and his wife, Marie Messick, founded their business, Taylor & Messick, in 1951. The longtime John Deere dealer has been a fixture on the Delmarva Peninsula since 1951 and continues to serve the public to this day. Located in Harrington, Delaware, right down the road from the Delaware State Fairgrounds, Taylor & Messick has been a staple sponsor of racers and racing in Delaware since its inception. Walt Messick's son and general manager of Taylor & Messick, Jimmy Messick, remembers his dad's love of racing and how he first got involved.

> *Dad started years ago at the Harrington track that ran Micro Midgets. They used to race at Blackbird and at Harry Greenburg's track that was located where Atlantic Concrete is now in Harrington. He would run Midgets, and they were powered by Indian motors back at that time. It just kind of escalated from there. He got involved later on with Norris "Speedy" Reed, because Speedy was a farmer and they did a lot of business together. He sponsored a lot of his cars, from Modifieds all the way up to when they ran NASCAR. Mom and Dad just loved to go to races. It was a top priority at our place to make the races. If someone wanted to buy five combines, Dad would say, "I have got to go to the races right now, but I will talk to you tomorrow." That is just how important racing was to him.*

Taylor & Messick always had a huge presence at the Delaware State Fair, and the racetrack at the fair was no exception.

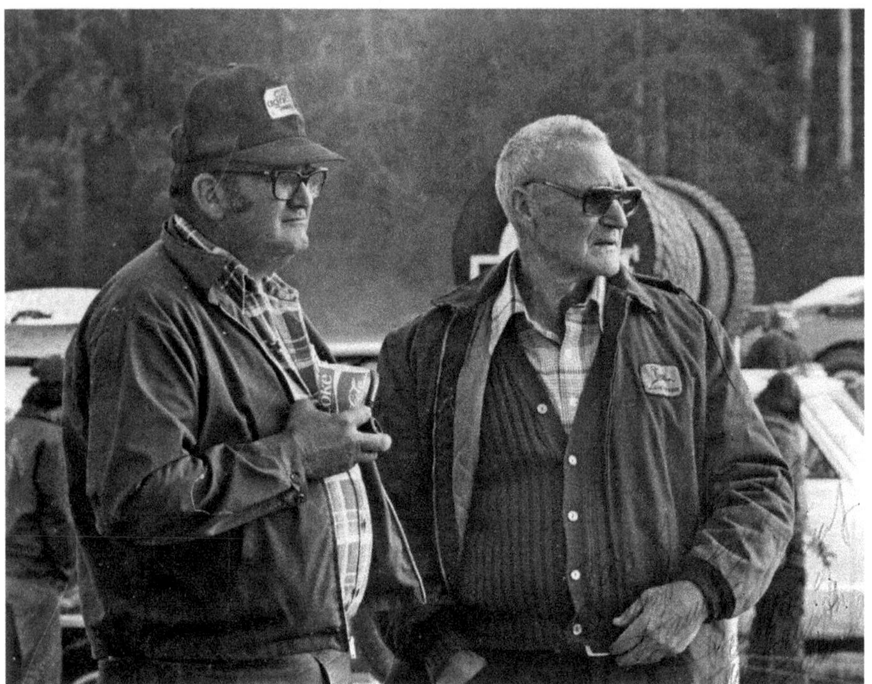

Two giants of auto racing in Delaware: Norris "Speedy" Reed (*left*) and Walt Messick (*right*). *Courtesy of Jimmy Messick.*

> *Dad was heavily involved in the racing at the Delaware State Fairgrounds. There are photos of when Sam Nunis would come to promote races at the Fairgrounds, and every truck on the speedway to push off the cars is a Taylor & Messick truck. He was the wheelman at the fair for a very long time and made things happen around that place. Dad and Tom Brown ran all the fire company races at the speedway in which the proceeds went to help buy fire equipment for the local fire company. He would go through Bill France to get the insurance for the races at that time. I remember those times. It was a lot of work getting that horse track ready for cars to race on. I remember Dad, Tom Brown and our neighbor Frankie Hendricks would all get together and go out at nighttime and put calcium on the track. It was a big deal.*

Auto racing on a track that was made for horse racing always provided its own set of challenges, but there is no doubt that the races at the Delaware State Fair was one of the year's most prestigious and highly anticipated events. While many local racers complained about the racing surface, they would still show up for an opportunity to race in front of the massive crowds that attended each year's event.

> *It was just a special place to race. The drivers would complain about the surface, but they would all be there when we opened the gate. It was just like going to the Daytona 500 in a lot of ways for our local dirt drivers. Dad was a promoter, fan, sponsor and owner, and when an event like the fair races came along, sometimes he was all four of those in one night.*

Perhaps one of the most well-known and memorable cars that Walt Messick sponsored in his years was the no. 1 Modified driven by Walt Breeding and owned by Speedy Reed. Although cars changed looks and chassis manufacturers through the years, the memorable yellow car with a stars and stripes no. 1 grabbed fans' attention wherever it went. Whether a Late Model or a Modified, you were guaranteed that more often than not the no. 1 would win or be near the front by the end of the night. One of the most memorable rides fans remember was the radically offset Kenny

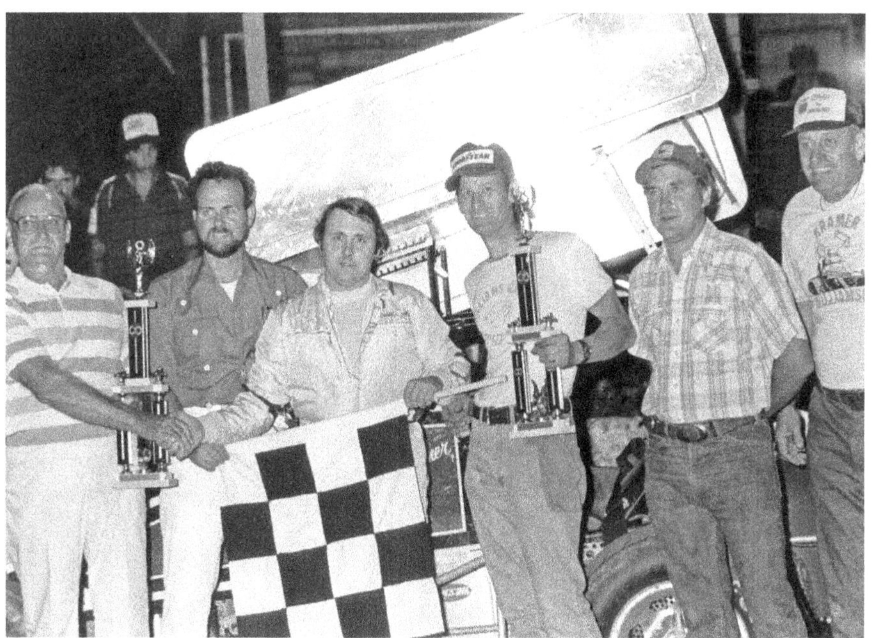

A fan of all types of racing, Walt Messick shakes the hand of Sprint Car driver Kramer Williamson. *Courtesy of Sharon Williamson.*

Weld–built chassis that Walt Breeding drove with great success on the East Coast. Jimmy Messick remembers the mutual admiration that his dad and car owner Speedy Reed had for each other.

> *They had a great relationship and a great rapport. Everybody was happy most of the time. It was not like today, where it is a cut-throat type deal. For example, an owner might say, "Well you had your name on my car for two races, you owe me some money." It was never like that with them. They just put the name on the car and went racing! They were just really good friends. They felt the same way about Walt, too. They all just got along so well.*

There is no way to measure the impact that Walt Messick had on racing in the Delaware area. But we do know there would be a large void and racing would have been much different in the First State if it had not been for the many contributions he made to the sport as a fan, owner, promoter and sponsor. Racing is all about passion, and perhaps no one had more passion for racing than Walt and Marie Messick. Look around the track today and you will see the Taylor & Messick name sponsoring many races. Son Jimmy carries on the tradition of his parents by actively sponsoring races and race series today. Recently, a section of grandstands at Delaware International Speedway was named after the Messicks for their dedication to motorsports—a fitting tribute to a great racing family.

21

THE RUST BROTHERS

For the Rust brothers, life has always been about racing. Brothers Duane and the late Deron Rust have long been a fixture on the racing scene. As with many families involved in racing, it all started when the boys were young, according to their mother, Irene.

> *Their uncle Lou Johnson kept his race car at our place for a bit, so they were exposed to racing at an early age and just fell in love with it. Lou's number was no. 96 so they both made it part of their numbers in racing as a tribute. Duane was no. 296 and Deron was no. 396. The boys both grew up to be racers and had their own specialties. Duane was the motor man. He did the engines and was very good at it. Deron was the fabricator. He was always coming up with unique ideas for the cars, and his work was beautiful.*

The brothers have raced in both premier divisions in Delaware. Records at Delaware International Speedway show that Duane Rust notched five feature wins in the Late Model class. Duane now races in the Crate Modified class in a tribute car that bears a combination of his no. 296 and his late brother Deron's no. 396.

Deron Rust passed away in 2013 but left behind a lasting legacy on the track. Deron started racing in 1984 and showed much promise as a driver from the start. At Delaware International Speedway, he won seventeen features as well as the coveted Camp Barnes Race in 1989. His mother

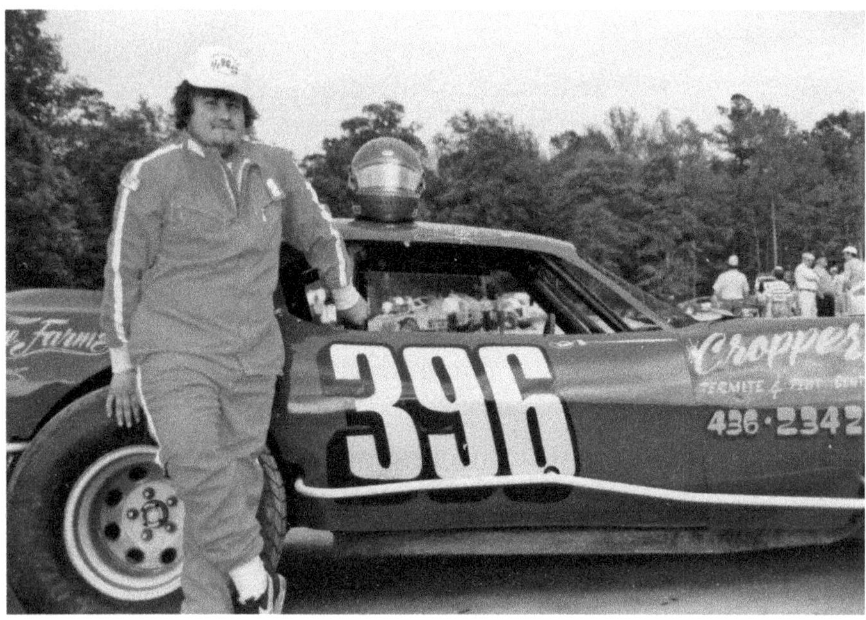

The late Deron Rust stands next to his no. 396 Late Model race car. *Courtesy of Don and Linda Allen, D&L Photos.*

talks about how much he loved racing and the lengths he would go to in order to attend a race.

> *Deron lived racing. He would eat, sleep and race. One time, we were at Hagerstown racing and we had a friend fly us back to Georgetown Airport so we could race again that night in Delaware. We lived right across from the airport so we literally walked from the runway over to our house and went to the track. Deron ended up winning that night. I would say his favorite win was the Small Block Modified race he won at Hagerstown. It was just a neat deal to travel up there and beat some of the best drivers and teams on the East Coast. That was a special win.*

Before his passing, Deron also played a pivotal role in helping Georgetown Speedway stay afloat during some rough times. Deron took over promotional duties and kept the gates open at the speedway. "He just had a dream and a vision for that speedway. He did not want it to sit there with the gates closed," says Irene Rust. Perhaps more than the legacy Deron left from his driving career, most will remember him for helping keep the gates of Georgetown Speedway open and helping launch the track back into the success it is today. Longtime racing photographer Don Allen had these words to say about Deron after his passing.

> *Deron Rust truly lived for racing. If it is true that "dirt trackin" gets in our blood, then his blood was racing fuel, motor oil and clay. He learned the sport at the knee of his uncle Lou Johnson and brought that same competitive spirit every race night. In his short time as a promoter, his knowledge and love of our sport successfully kept our beloved Georgetown Speedway alive for two more seasons. Working with him and his family during that time will remain one of my most cherished memories, and I know that if he were still with us, he would be so happy to see the rebirth of Georgetown Speedway and the success of Brett Deyo. Deron would probably be trying for a Short Track Super Series Championship.*

While some families shy away from racing, its dangers and commitments, Irene Rust was glad both of her boys got involved in the sport.

> *I am so proud of both boys and how they always took time for the kids at the races and outside the track. Sometimes they would take their cars to*

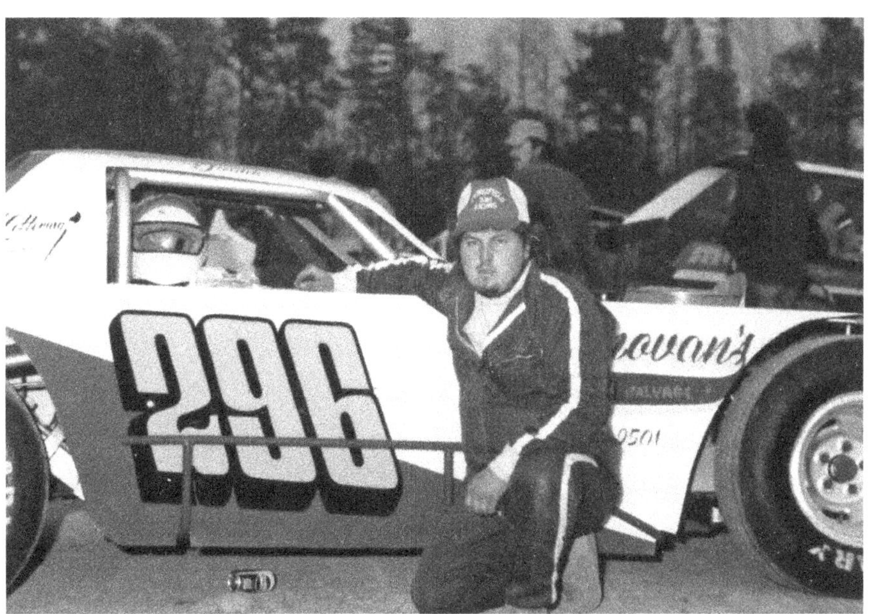

The other half of the Rust brother duo, Duane Rust, poses next to his Late Model car before the night's action. *Courtesy of Don and Linda Allen, D&L Photos.*

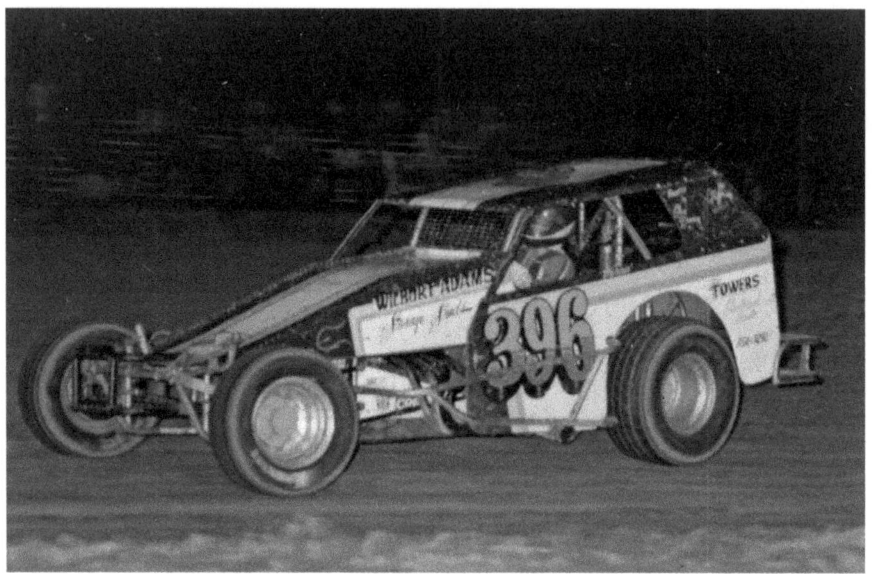

Deron Rust loved to race anything with wheels, and he also raced in the Modified division. *Courtesy of Don and Linda Allen, D&L Photos.*

> *show young children the sport. It has been a wonderful journey. Both boys loved racing. Although we spent a lot of time and money, it always gave them something to do; they never had time to get into trouble; all of their energy was focused on racing.*

The Rust family continues to support Georgetown Speedway, and the track now hosts the Deron Rust Memorial Race every year to remember the contributions made by Deron to racing and his passion for the speedway. Irene and Duane Rust still carry on the family tradition of looking after the kids at the races, as they often donate and give away a bicycle at the yearly event.

22

RICHARD JARVIS

1945-2017

The late Richard Jarvis was well known throughout racing as a true competitor who raced wide open all the time. Often running the cushion or the high groove on the track, Jarvis made many fans throughout his racing career. For many years, the no. 680 Modified race car was a staple at Delaware International and Georgetown Speedways. Richard's son Richard Jarvis Jr. tells about his dad's early love of cars and how the no. 680 came to be.

> *Dad always had a love of fast cars. When he was younger, he would always help out on his brother-in-law's drag car. He had several run-ins with the law for driving too fast on the road, so I guess racing just was a good fit for him. The no. 68 on his race car came from my sister, Shelly. That was the year she was born, so that was the number he ran. When he teamed up with Darrell "Boogie" Hitchens, the number changed to no. 680. Boogie was always no. 80, so they just combined the two numbers together to form no. 680, and that stuck for the rest of his career in Dirt Modified. He would go back to the no. 68 in the NASCAR Sportsman Series.*

After serving his country at a young age in the National Guard, Jarvis returned home and began his work in the construction industry. Starting as a carpenter, Jarvis began to supervise and run different construction projects before he turned twenty years old. Working in and around the Ocean

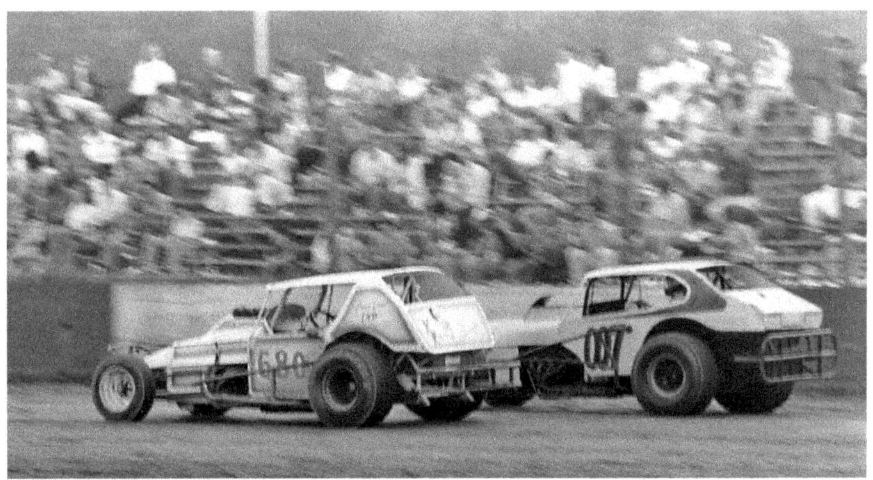

Richard Jarvis in the no. 680 battles with Ron Tobias in the no. 007. *Author's collection.*

City, Maryland area, Jarvis went on to become a partner in the successful Purnell-Jarvis Inc., one of the area's top builders specializing in motels and condominiums. The company's logo would become a familiar sight as a sponsor on the side of Richard's race cars. Although Richard Jarvis became a successful entrepreneur and racer, the success never went to his head. He was well known for his generosity to those in need, and there are many stories in the area of times when Richard lent a hand when needed to make a difference.

Racing during a time when there were so many top teams running Delaware International and Georgetown Speedways, Jarvis became known as a front-runner. Becoming well known in his Olsen Eagle Chassis, Jarvis won twenty-nine features and the 1981 Track Championship at Delaware International Speedway against the best drivers of the era. Richard Jarvis Jr. recalls his dad's driving style and some of his favorite races.

> *Dad was really proud of the Syracuse Qualifier he won. Winning the race guaranteed a starting spot at the big race, so he was really proud of that. The other race he talked about a lot was one he didn't actually win. It was the big National Race at Nazareth. He would tell the story about him running second and the track was only one groove, so there was very little passing. He could stay put and run second or try to pass on the outside. Well, Dad was always going to go for it. That was just his style. I think he ended up around fifth place or something that day, but he was not complacent to run around in second; he was going to try something to win.*

Jarvis remained a fixture in the Modified ranks until the early 1990s, when he decided to try his skills on the NASACR Igloo Sportsman Challenge Series. Jarvis enjoyed his time racing in the series until a serious wreck at Pocono Speedway in Pennsylvania sidelined him and his car. As the wreck of the car was sitting in the garage waiting to be fixed, Richard Jarvis Jr. started to take a liking to racing, just like his dad. Some Karts were bought, and the torch was passed from father to son. Richard Jarvis never raced again but was just as happy watching his son become involved in the sport he loved so much. Richard Jarvis Jr. would carve out his own legacy in racing, winning three national championships in various Kart classes early in his career. Early success helped Jarvis Jr. move up in race classes at a quick pace. After years of honing his driving skills in various classes, Jarvis Jr. found a home in the super competitive Late Model division, where the no. 680 would once again be at the forefront of racing in Delaware. Winning twenty-six races at Delaware International Speedway and the 2009 Track Championship, Jarvis Jr. has carried forward the winning ways established by his father.

Successful not only at the racetrack, Richard Jarvis Jr. now follows his father's footsteps in his profession as well. Jarvis Jr. works in the construction

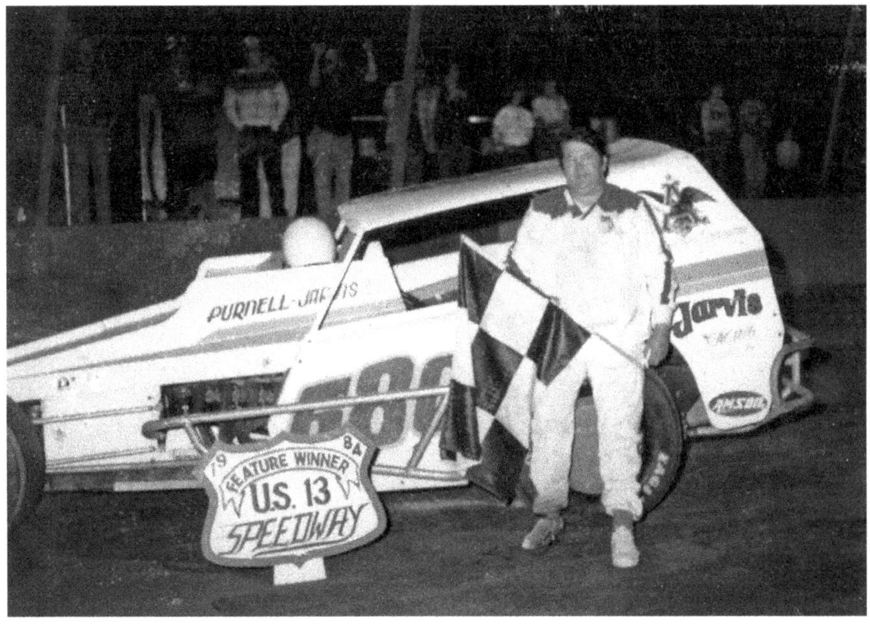

Richard Jarvis had a great 1984 season in his Olsen Eagle chassis at US 13 Speedway in Delmar, Delaware. *Courtesy of Don and Linda Allen, D&L Photos.*

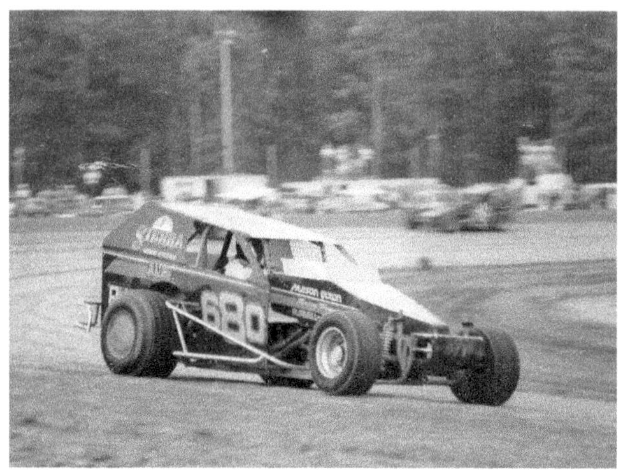

A rare photo of Richard Jarvis driving for owner Gerald Banks and his Mason-Dixon Racing Team. *Author's collection.*

and development industry and carries on the tradition of excellence established by his father. With the passing of Richard Jarvis Sr. in late 2017, area racing lost a true giant. Jarvis is gone but not forgotten. Fans will long remember the flat-out driving style and the white and blue no. 680 Olsen Eagle Modified sliding sideways around the corners for years to come.

23
MELVIN JOSEPH JR.

Racing a car was all Melvin Joseph Jr. ever wanted to do. From the very beginning, Melvin was surrounded by racing. "Little Mel," or Mel Jr., as people often refer to him, was the son of the late Melvin Joseph, who fielded race cars for years and built both Georgetown and Dover International Speedways. Growing up in a racing family certainly made an impression on Mel Jr. as a young child, and he remembers that those early times had a great influence on him.

> *I pretty much grew up at the track. I was at the beach at Daytona in 1955 when my dad's car won, and then I was at every single race at the beach until the big speedway opened in 1959. Dad's Modified car also won that very first race at the super speedway. All I can remember was that racing was all I ever wanted to do. Then, when I was around three years old, Dad told me that if I would eat better he would buy me a quarter midget race car. I was always so tiny and frail, they were looking for ways to get me to eat better. So that was pretty much the start of it all. I ran quarter midgets and then flat track motorcycles. I did not tell my parents I was doing that. My friends would come by and take me to the track. When I was a teenager, I ran Karts. I had no clue what I was doing, but I was fortunate enough to win a few races. Then, I had a friend move here from New Jersey with his parents, and we decided we were going to build a race car. Neither one of us had ever built anything, but we had our minds set on building a car. So, we built a car and went racing at Little Lincoln. The car was no. 13, and*

my dad did not know I was running a race car initially. We hid the car and we used my friend's name, Robert Cunningham, as the driver, but it was really me driving. I drove a right good while, and then one night I got out of the car after I won and there was my dad standing there. I was floored! I mean, you could have bought me for a nickel right then. He wanted to know if I was ashamed of my name, since I was using someone else's name, and I told him no, but I did not think he would let me race. He said that I was right, but I told him I was eighteen now and he said, "Well you can keep the car at the shop, but it will have to be outside at night, but before you do that the number has to be changed." He would not allow anything with a 13 on it near the yard. He asked me where in the world did I come up with the number 13. Dad's racing number was of course no. 49, so I told him that 4 and 9 equals 13 and that is where I came up with the number. The six-cylinders and eight-cylinders all ran together back then with the six-cylinders starting up front. We had a Ford Falcon station wagon at first that I bought off of Bill Lawson. Those were good times, and I learned a great deal back then.

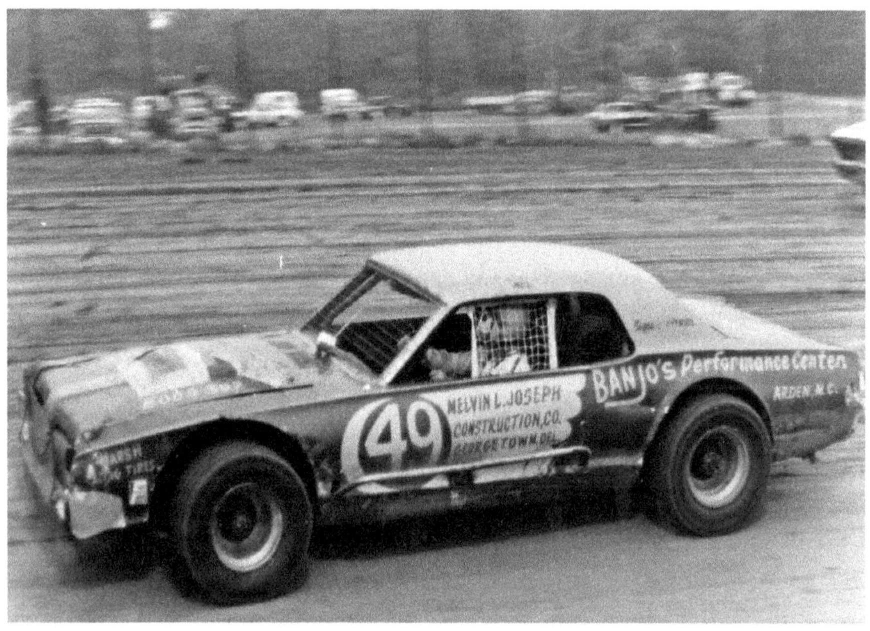

Melvin Joseph Jr. in one of his early Ford-powered cars sponsored by NASCAR legend Banjo Matthews. *Courtesy of Melvin Joseph Jr.*

Over his long career, Mel Jr. has raced in many divisions, including Late Models, Limited Late Models, Dwarf Cars, Little Lincolns and Modifieds. Most fans will remember his domination of the Limited Late Model class for years at both Delaware International and Georgetown Speedways. For years, Mel Jr. gave Ford fans something to root for as his orange no. 49 Mustang was often the only Ford in the field and, more often than not, was at the front. Mel Jr. was not just a great driver; he also had a firm grasp on how to get the absolute maximum performance out of a rather stock car as compared to the other classes. Looking back on a career that included a win total in the triple digits, Mel Jr. counts his wins at the Delaware State Fairgrounds in Harrington as among his most important.

> *I never kept a record of how many times I won. The only notes I kept were how to set the car up. I would say that the wins at the State Fair were right up at the top. Being the overall winner there was special. I won on both nights many times to win the overall title. The fair was a unique track, and it either suited you or it did not. Believe it or not, I think my time running motorcycles on flat tracks with cinders really helped me at the fairgrounds.*

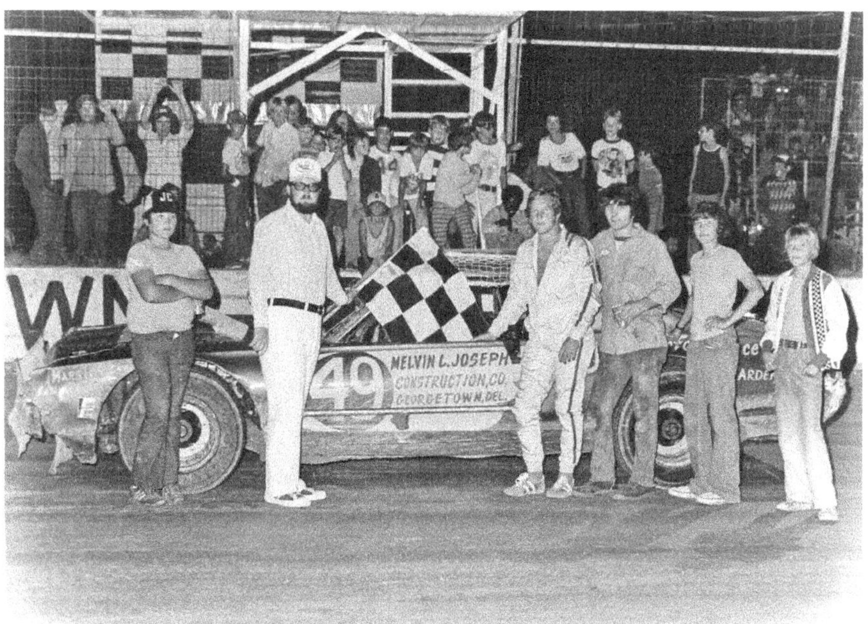

The no. 49 Ford of Melvin Joseph parked in Victory Lane at Georgetown Speedway. *Courtesy of Melvin Joseph Jr.*

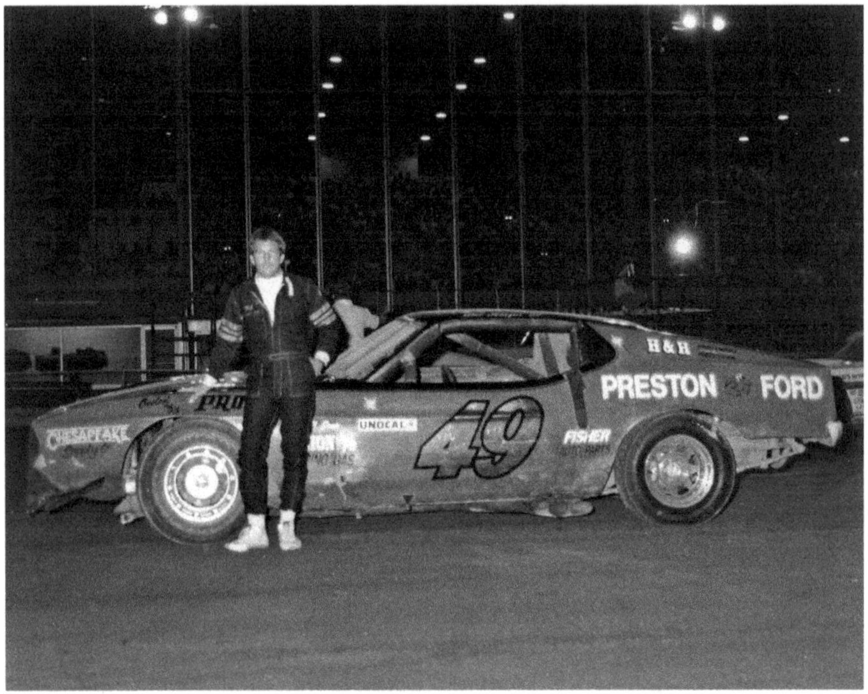

Melvin Joseph Jr. next to his no. 49 Ford Mustang in front of a capacity crowd at the Delaware State Fairgrounds. *Courtesy of Melvin Joseph Jr.*

> *You could not even show the accelerator a picture of your shoe. That was just how gentle you had to be with the throttle. We always extended the throttle linkage for that race because of the slick nature of the track. That made it uncomfortable to get the pedal to the floor.*

Today, Mel Jr. still enjoys competing in his no. 49 Little Lincoln race car, often at the front of the pack competing for the win. His other favorite pastime is enjoying his grandkids and watching races at the nearby Club Milton Speedway. Joseph's grandson Gavin is moving up to Outlaw Quarter Midgets after a few successful years in the Bandit division, ensuring that the no. 49 will be a familiar sight at the track for years to come.

24

HAROLD BUNTING

When I set out on writing this book and interviewing the many racers that are featured in these pages, I would always ask the question, Who was the toughest competitor that you ever raced against from Delaware? More often than not, the name that rose to the top of the list was Harold Bunting. Bunting will always be known as one of the smartest and toughest drivers to ever sit behind the wheel of a race car. Fellow Modified competitor Billy Towers, who raced with Bunting for some time, recalls his style of racing.

> *I like Harold and I think he liked me as well, but on the track, he would not give you an inch, not an inch! He reminded me a lot of another top racer, Danny Johnson. He would try you every corner of every lap. He was just relentless and he knew sooner or later you were going to make a mistake and he would capitalize on that. He never just rode behind someone unless he was stalking you, but once he figured out where your weakness was he attacked. Just relentless pressure! Harold was just a good, clean driver. He came to race and win every time. He was not there to party or make friends; he came to race. I never will forget this saying he had. He always said, "I bring my friends with me," and he was serious. He wasn't there to make friends on the track; he came to win. He was serious, and you have to give him a lot of credit for that. He had some good rides as well, but his driving style and ability commanded good equipment, and he certainly made the best out of it.*

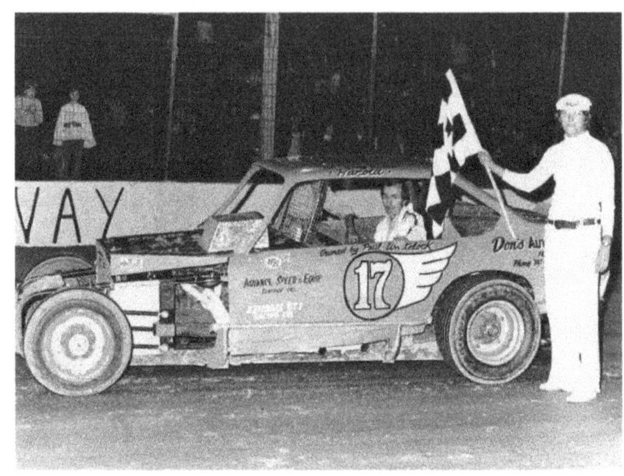

Harold Bunting celebrates another victory in the Paul Whitlock–owned no. 17. *Courtesy of the Whitelock family*.

Like most racers, Harold Bunting cut his teeth in the racing world on the kart tracks of southern Delaware before jumping into a full-size race car. His journey to the driver's seat was helped along by fellow racer and racing legend Harry Dutton, as Harold Bunting explains in his own words.

> *I was working at the Ford garage with Harry Dutton's brother, Harvey Dutton. I was racing Karts at the time, and Harvey said, "Why don't you go down to Harry's and help him with his race car; he could use some help with it." So that is what I did. I started to go down and regularly help him work on the car. So one Saturday, we were coming back from the races, and Harry said, "I don't think I want to drive anymore; you can drive next week; I have won enough." Harry had won like six races in a row at the time, and I thought he was joking, but he surely was not. He put me in his car at Little Lincoln and in my first feature, I ran in the back of someone and busted the radiator. Harry never said a word. Harry was right easygoing and quiet unless you made him mad, then you had your hands full. So we loaded it up, went home and repaired it for the following week by putting in a new radiator. We went back the next week, and I did the exact same thing over again, busted the radiator by running into the back of another car. This time, we were hauling the car home and everything was quiet. We both had not said a word, and just as we made our turn at Ellendale to head toward Milton, Harry said, "Well, I got one more damn radiator; you break it and you're done." I said "OK!" Then Harry said, "Look! Let me tell you something. You win everything with those Go-Karts, but you're driving looking at your nose; you need to look up over your hood." Certainly good advice. That first car was a 1955 red Ford no. 888.*

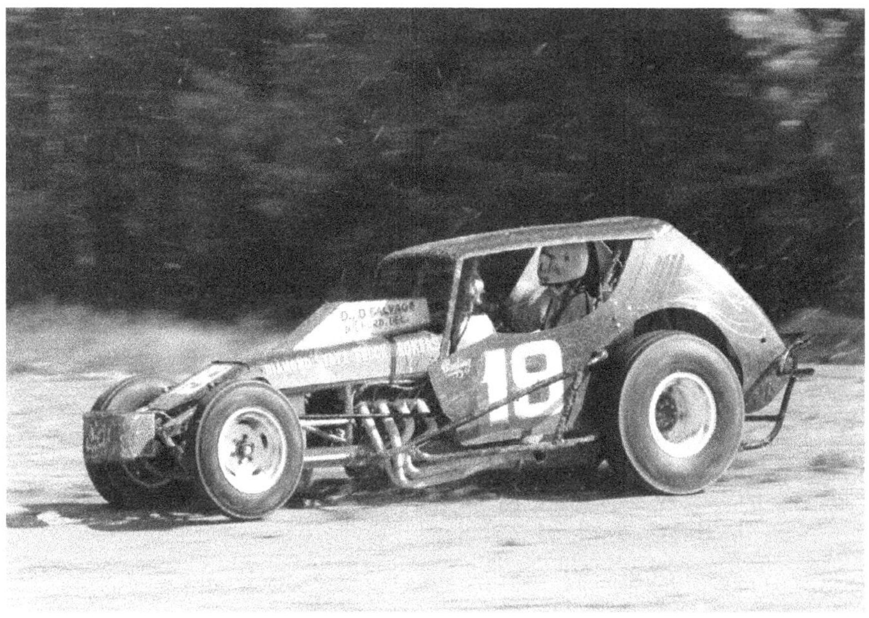

Piloting a Kenny Weld Chassis Modified for owner Steve Dale at US 13 Speedway is driver Harold Bunting. *Courtesy of Harold Bunting.*

After getting his start driving for Harry Dutton, Bunting went on to drive for some of the top car owners in the area. Driving for owners like Whitelock, Warrington, Mills and Dale Bunting, he made a name for himself as the area's top Modified pilot, winning hundreds of features along the way. A racer's racer, Bunting never had a favorite victory or a favorite track.

> *The tracks are all round and a win is a win. I enjoyed all the tracks from US 13, where you have a ton of grip, to the Harrington Fair, where you really had to hook your head and foot together to control the car because of the loose track. That was always a fun track. You had to drive like you had an egg under the accelerator, and a lot of my competitors just never could do that at the fair, and that is why we were so successful at that track. Everybody was just so used to being able to stand on the gas at all the other tracks and you just could not do that at the fairgrounds and be successful.*

From the 1970s until 1986, Harold Bunting's name would be at the forefront of Modified racing. He established his reputation as one of the racers to beat in a Modified car. Not only a first-class driver, Bunting was also a first-class engine builder. He explains what it took to build an engine to compete on the unique Delaware-area tracks.

> *We always had good motors. We did not spend much on them, but we always had some of the best running motors in the field. For racing around here, the engines needed to be different. The reason our engines ran so well is because I raced down here and a lot of these other engine builders were from up around New York and Pennsylvania. They just did not know what getting a hold of a track was like. Because down here in Delaware, the tracks especially back when I was racing were heavy, and when running those old drag tires you just could not have enough power to get off the corners. They put milder cams in their engines so they would pull easy and not break loose on the track. Those engines would really not hit their stride until the middle of the straightaway. When I built an engine, I built it to try to pull a tree stump out of the ground, because that is what you need to get off the corners down here.*

Harold Bunting ended his racing career in 1986, going out on his own terms and winning the Delaware International Speedway Track Championship at year's end, driving for owner Steve Dale in the no. 19D D&D Dismantling Modified. Bunting raced the last three years of his career for owner Steve Dale, a time when he enjoyed much of his success. Bunting tells the story of how the two first met.

> *Steve bought a lot of cars from where I worked. Fred Workman and Harvey Dutton, who I worked with and was good friends with, talked Steve into buying a Modified, and Fred was driving it. While they were racing that car, I was driving for Dutch Warrington. He had just bought me a brand-new Kenny Weld chassis. Not too long after that, Dutch had a heart attack, and we just parked the car. While recovering, he told me that he was not going to field a car for a while and if I could find someone to buy the car. Steve came into the dealership one day, and Fred was not doing too good at the time with the car. Harvey was a Ford man, and they had a Holman-Moody 429 ci engine, and for whatever reason they just were not going really good at that time. Steve came in, and I said, "Hey, why don't you buy a winning car." He just looked at me and said, "What?" I told him Dutch was not going to be able to race for some time and that Weld car was for sale.*

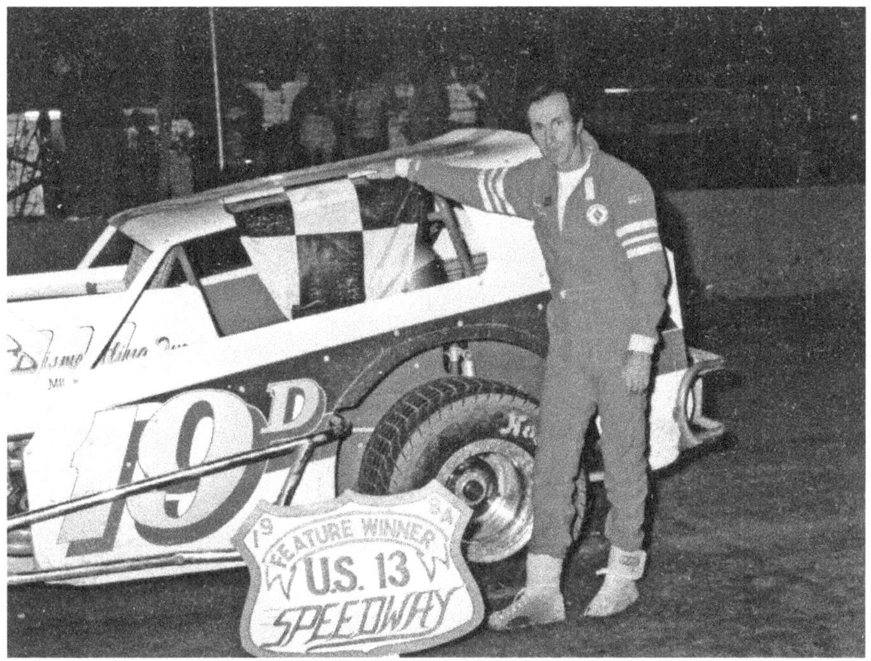

During the later years of his driving career, Harold Bunting had much success behind the wheel of the no. 19D Modified. *Courtesy of Don and Linda Allen, D&L Photos.*

> *Davis Concrete was a really good friend of Steve's, and Steve did a lot of work for them, and Mike Cole, who had a trucking company, was real good friends with him as well. After a few days of thinking about it, Steve and those guys went together and bought that Weld car, and that is how we first got started. We ran for a short time before I ran for a few other owners, but we got back together for the last three years of my racing career to win a bunch of races.*

Throughout his career, Bunting credits those who worked behind the scenes as a reason for his success on the track.

> *We always had some of the best help around. We worked many of a night, and those guys hung right in there and never complained. We worked a many of an hour to get the success we had on the track. Guys like Painter Lynch, Jim Hayes, Mark West and Marvin Mitchell all worked countless hours to make sure we had the best car possible when we hit the track.*

Bunting's quiet, no-nonsense nature made him one of the most feared, intimidating and respected drivers ever to come from Delaware. His love of racing has been passed on to his son H.J. Bunting, who has had an equally impressive career, winning races and championships in the Modified ranks. H.J. continues to be one of the top drivers today and carries on the Bunting winning tradition. To this day, stories are still told of Harold Bunting's exploits on the track. History will remember Mr. Bunting as a competitor who was laser-focused on winning and was one of the smartest, most competitive drivers to ever sit behind the wheel.

25

HAL BROWNING

In a career that spanned fifty-four years, Hal Browning was a familiar name up and down the Mid-Atlantic. Browning raced and won in almost every class of car from the age of twenty-one until finally hanging up his helmet at the age of seventy-four. His longevity was impressive, but when you consider his competitiveness and that the winning continued as he raced into his seventies, you have the makings of a legend. Not bad for a guy who learned how to drive a race car in his in-laws' apple orchard.

> *I was twenty-one years old when I started racing. At that time, they would not let you start racing until you were that age. I never even witnessed a race until I was about eighteen years old. I went with my brother-in-law to watch and I was like, "Man, I really have to get one of them race cars." I bought an old race car from a junkyard and put a motor in it. I could not race it because I was not twenty-one yet, so I drove it around my future father-in-law's apple orchard and tore a bunch of trees up. I also drove it up and down the road just playing and practicing with it. When I moved to the Baltimore area, I bought an old Studebaker and began my racing career at Westport Stadium in Baltimore, Maryland. I knew right away that is what I wanted to do, and I did exactly that for fifty-four years.*

Before becoming a regular fixture at the speedways in Delaware, Browning raced at some of the most legendary tracks in Maryland and Pennsylvania. He raced everything from Coupes and Bugs to Modifieds and

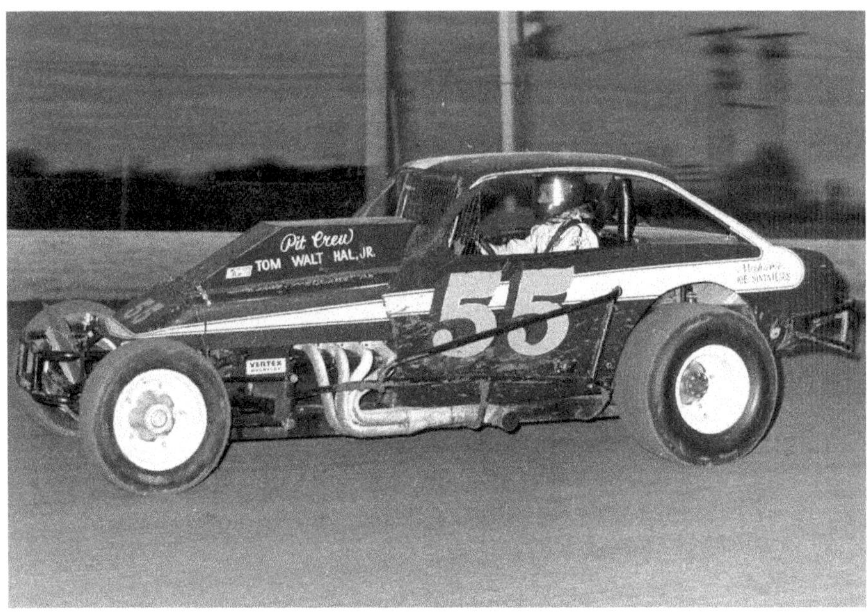

Hal Browning was a threat to win, no matter what class he was driving in. Browning is shown here in one of his early no. 55 Modifieds. *Author's collection.*

Late Models, and even Sprint Cars, at tracks like Westport Stadium, Dorsey Speedway, Lincoln Speedway, Reading Speedway, Susquehanna Speedway, Hagerstown Speedway and Williams Grove Speedway. Browning brought his winning ways to Delaware for the first time in the early 1970s.

> *I was living in Pennsylvania, and we went down to race in Delaware for the first time in 1972 or 1973. We went down to the end-of-the-year race at Georgetown Speedway. We actually won that race. It was a 101-lap race. Instead of 100 laps, it was 101, for the guys who were always complaining they could have done better if they had one more lap. After winning that race, we came back down for the end-of-the-year race at US 13 Speedway, but we did not do very well at that one. It was a few years after that we started to run on a regular basis in Delaware. We just really liked the area and the tracks. I really liked US 13 at that time. It was always a heavy track and just a really good track. Georgetown was fun as well. It was a little bit bigger and a little bit faster, and everyone liked to go faster, but US 13 was just really consistent. You knew Charlie Cathell was going to have that track about the same each week.*

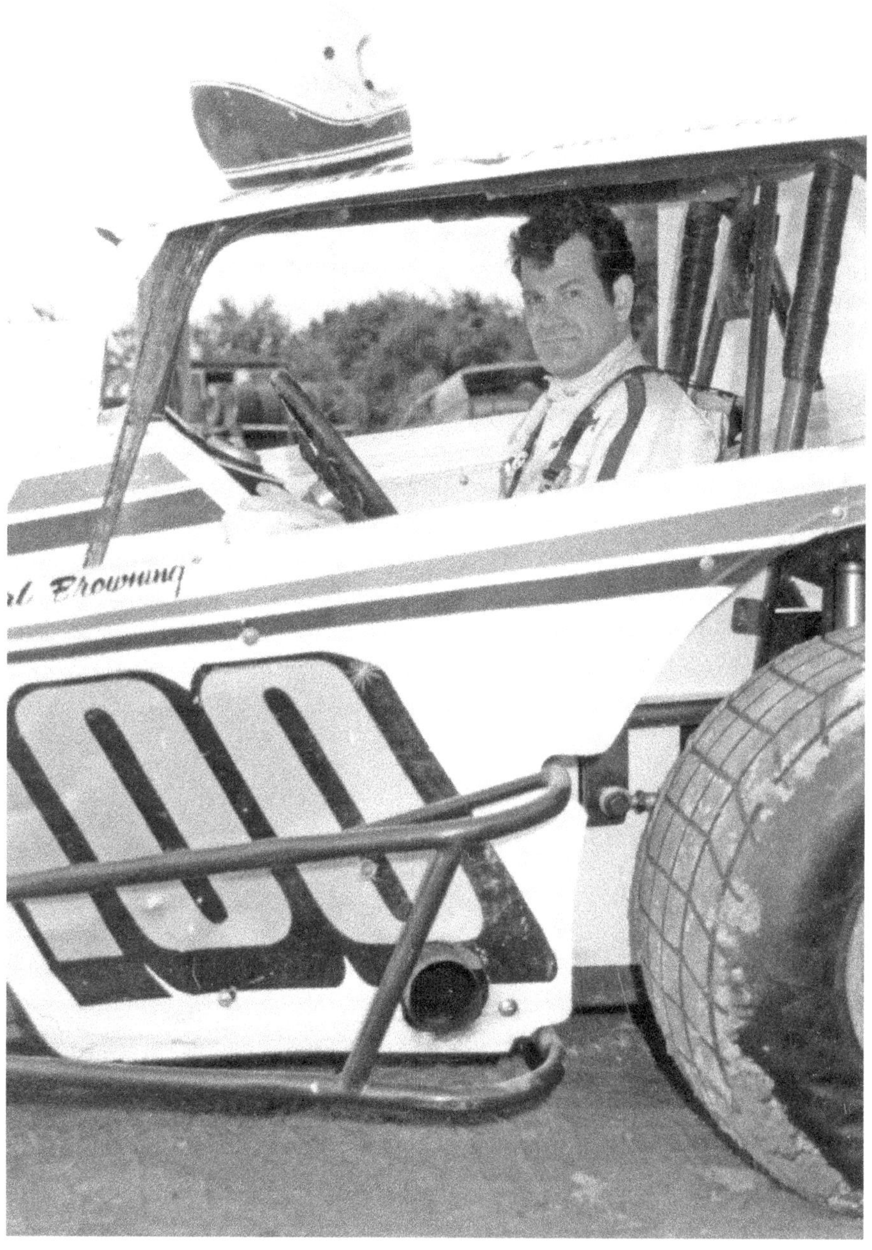

The always versatile Hal Browning strapping in his Modified, getting ready to head out on the track in the no. 100. *Courtesy of Don and Linda Allen, D&L Photos.*

Browning always had a special place in his heart for US 13 Speedway, which is now called Delaware International Speedway. During a one-off show late in his career, Browning shattered the old track record and set a new record at Delaware International. On May 22, 2010, during a special show that allowed the use of any kind of wings on the cars to aid in the handling, Browning, at the age of seventy-three, shattered the track record. His fastest lap on the tight half-mile dirt oval was 16.936 seconds, for a 106.282 mph average.

> *That was a fun night. That was the next to last year I raced. I was seventy-three, I guess. I could almost hold the throttle down the whole lap. I just had to burp the throttle just a bit to get the car to turn, and then you could get back in it. It was awesome and so much fun. I wish they did that every week. It was just a whole lot of fun.*

Those who witnessed Browning that night realized that the seventy-three-year-old was truly ageless and still at the top of his game, doing what he loved best, race cars. With all the types of cars Browning raced, you would think he may have a favorite type of car that suited his style best, but Browning says otherwise:

> *I enjoyed driving them all, Modifieds, Late Models and Sprint Cars. It is hard to say which was my favorite. Once we put wings on the Sprint Cars, I thought those were the easiest to drive. Sprint Cars at that time were so small, and after getting out of a Modified, getting in a Sprint Car was pretty much like straddling the motor. They were a whole lot smaller back then. The Bugs I raced back then were thirty inches wide and ninety inches long. That was the only rule they had, then eventually, the Bugs changed into Sprints.*

Browning would eventually move and become a full-time Delaware resident in 1980 and a regular at Delaware International , Georgetown and Harrington Speedways during the state fair. Most will remember Browning in his no. 100 race car owned by Alfred Parker. Browning achieved most of his success in Delaware with the team based at Cabbage Corner in Georgetown, Delaware.

> *I think we won championships in 1980 and 1982 in the no. 100 Hemi-powered car at Delaware International Speedway. Racing for Alfred Parker*

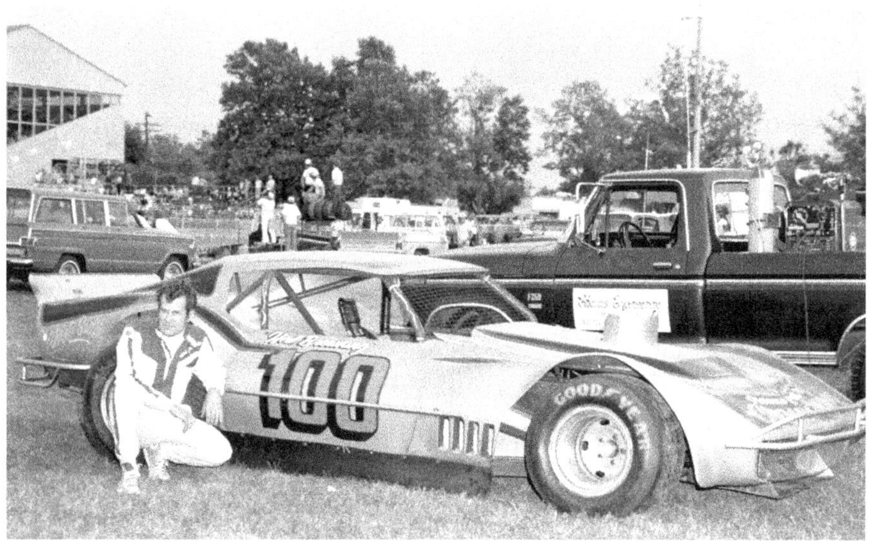

Hall Browning posing next to his Corvette-bodied Late Model in front of the grandstands at the Delaware State Fair. *Courtesy of Don and Linda Allen, D&L Photos.*

> *was really my best experience racing in Delaware. They were good people, and everything was homemade. Instead of just buying a car like today, those guys made everything they could for the car themselves. We ran just about everywhere we wanted, and although we did not win all the time, by our results, everyone knew we were there and we still won our fair share.*

Today, the ageless Browning still works driving a truck and attends the races every chance he gets. Looking like a man half his age, you can still see a sparkle in his eye when he is at the track watching a race. Although his racing days have passed, you have to believe he could still climb in, tighten those belts and get the job done!

26
BOBBY WILKINS

One cannot mention racing in Delaware without the name Bobby Wilkins coming up. Arguably one of the most successful and talented racers ever to come out of the First State, Wilkins's statistics have stood the test of time, and he remains the winningest Modified driver of all time at Delaware International Speedway, with 118 victories. One of the only drivers to win in a Modified, Late Model and a Sprint Car, Wilkins's statistics read like a hall of fame resume: 121 wins at Delaware International Speedway, 118 in a Modified, 2 in a Late Model and 1 in a Sprint Car. Wilkins also notched an amazing 8 Delaware International Speedway Track Championships in the Modified division. At Delaware's Georgetown Speedway, Wilkins scored 2 championships and had 26 total wins, 24 Modified wins and 2 Late Model victories. At the state fairgrounds in Harrington, Delaware, Wilkins won 9 times, all in a Modified, earning the coveted Delaware State Fair Dirt Track Championship along the way. While Delaware is where Wilkins did most of his racing, he did venture to Bridgeport Speedway in New Jersey and earn 5 Modified victories and 1 Sprint Car win. Wilkins also earned 1 Modified Track Championship at Bridgeport in 1986. Despite his career success, Bobby never lost sight of where he came from and his humble beginnings in the local karting scene.

I started right out in karts. It was so popular around the Delaware area and especially in Milford because of events like the Milford Street Race. My dad was good friends with Harold Bunting, Sonny Brittingham and the

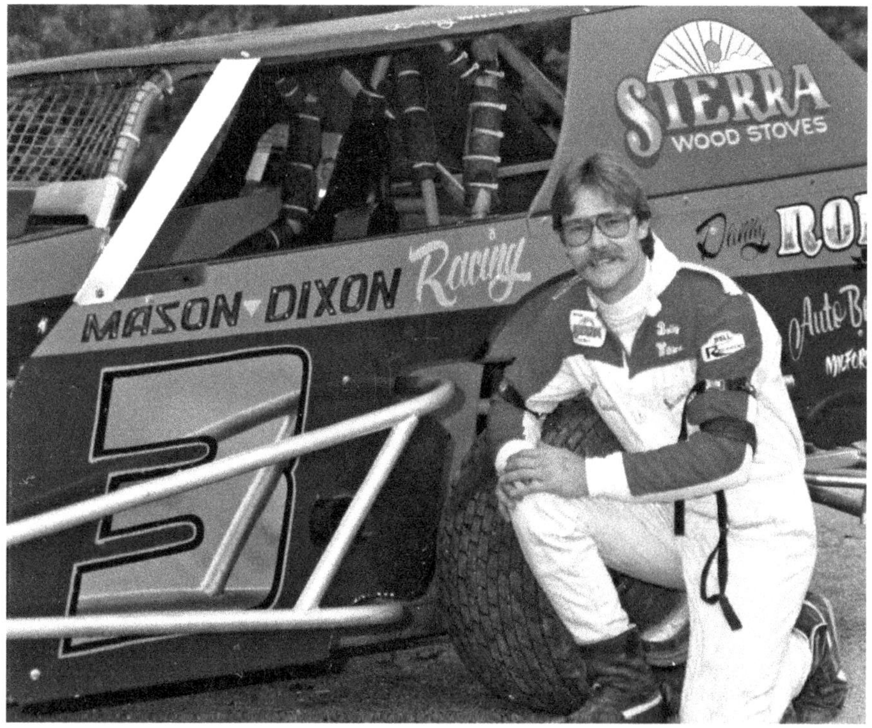

The winningest Modified driver in Delaware International Speedway's history, Bobby Wilkins. *Courtesy of Don and Linda Allen, D&L Photos.*

> *Carpenters, who had the dirt pit where we would race when we first started. It was such a family-oriented sport and a great way to learn the basics and work yourself up the ladder and into something bigger and faster.*

During his long career, Wilkins got to pilot some of the best cars in the area. Driving and winning for owners like Andy Anderson, Al Dillinger, Eugene Mills, Gerald Banks, Brian Gladden and Kelly Hastings, Wilkins earned a reputation for getting the most out of his equipment. It is his time driving the no. 19D for owner Steve Dale that fans remember the most. The greatest portion of Wilkins's career wins came behind the wheel of the Steve Dale–owned no. 19D Modified. Before earning the opportunity to race such coveted rides, Wilkins paid his dues learning and racing in some of the area's lower classes.

> *I raced at Little Lincoln when I was fifteen years old. My dad bought a car from the Lyons Brothers. Dad bought one of their Sportsman cars, which*

was a six-cylinder, and I raced it six times at Little Lincoln and I crashed it I think six times. Daddy then flat towed me to Georgetown Speedway and made me change all four tires with a lug wrench. I went out and qualified pretty good, so in the feature I had a decent starting position. But like the fifth lap my hood flipped up and I had to get towed in. Dad made me change the tires, and we came back home. Those were wild times.

Not just an accomplished driver, Wilkins was equally comfortable fabricating just about anything you could think of. Almost always involved in the construction of his car, Wilkins explains his love of being heavily involved with the design and building of the cars he raced. From constructing karts to his time at Hall of Fame Racing in North Carolina fabricating NASCAR race cars, Wilkins always had a love for the fabrication side of the sport.

I was very involved in all the chassis I drove. When it came down to it, I had just as much fun designing things for the car and seeing them come to life than winning with the car. When you build your own car and perform well, that is awesome, but when you build your own car and win, that is a feeling like no other. I really did not have a favorite car. The ultimate dirt-track racing is when I ran Sprint Cars. We did not have the funding to have an upper level engine program and compete up front, but between Andy Anderson and myself, we made the most of what we had and were able to win a few races. Obviously, I had great success with the Olsen Chassis cars. Of course, I drove them the longest and raced in many races with them. They were very comfortable cars that suited my driving style, and I was allowed to do many different things to those cars which helped their performance. I had so many ideas just from being around race cars all my life. I was lucky enough to know how a car felt and be able to make a change and feel that change in the performance of the car. It surprised me over the years what I learned in Kart racing and how it applied to all racing. From building karts, even though they did not have suspension, your suspension in karting was the tubing, I learned a lot what tubing could do. Well, tubing also is a factor in dirt cars and asphalt cars as well. I made a lot of friends through the fabrication part of the sport. I was fortunate and lucky enough to be around and learn from guys like Andy Anderson and Walt Breeding. Just being with those guys and learning about the chassis and then coupling that with my driving experience just helped to make me a better racer.

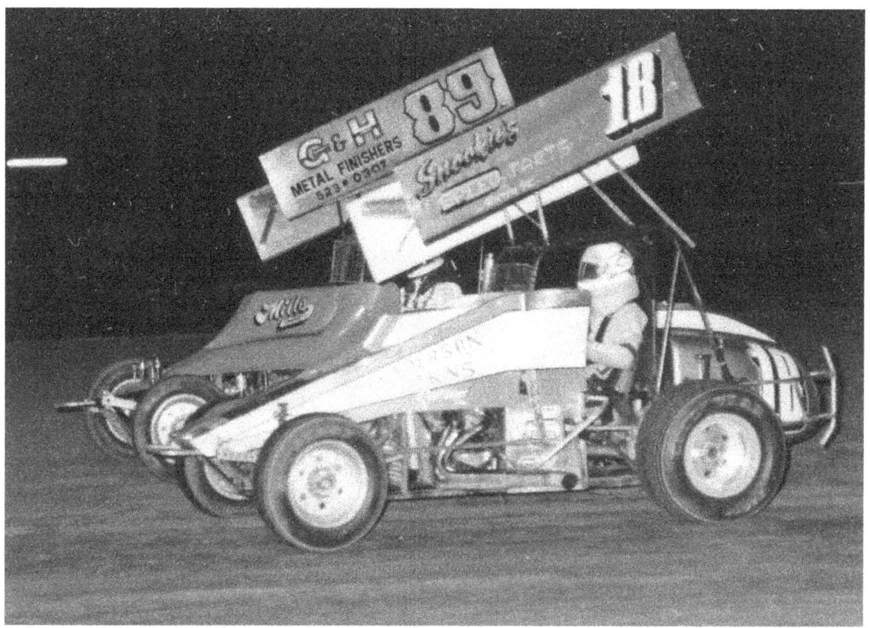

Bobby Wilkins was one of a select few drivers to win in Modifieds, Late Models and Sprint Cars. *Courtesy of Don and Linda Allen, D&L Photos.*

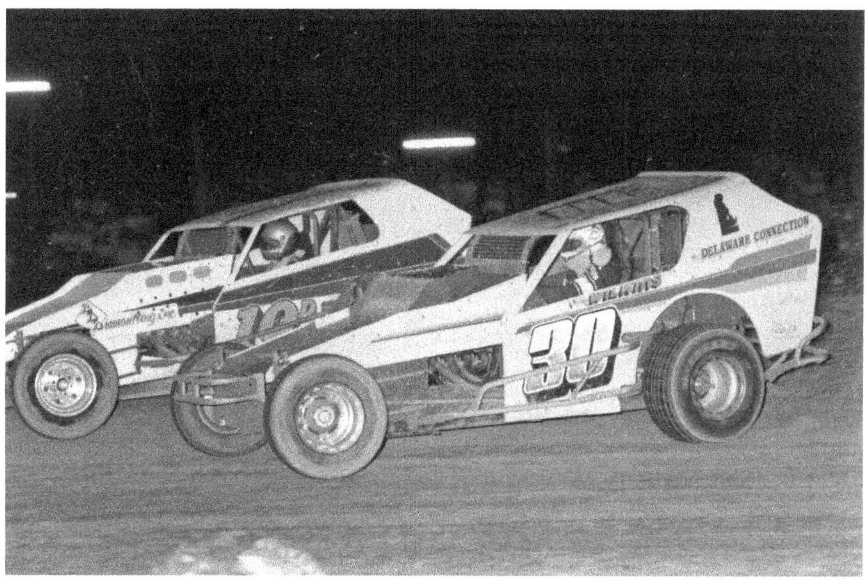

Bobby Wilkins in the no. 30 slides under the no. 19D of Harold Bunting. Wilkins also drove the no. 19D later in his career. *Courtesy of Don and Linda Allen, D&L Photos.*

Fans will remember Wilkins as a great racer, one who rewrote the record books and had fun doing it. Bobby's son Beau Wilkins follows in his dad's footsteps. Not just an excellent Modified racer, Beau is also an excellent fabricator like his father. One cannot help but notice the parallel history of the father and the son. Both have driven and won in Big Block Modifieds, both have worked for some of the top NASCAR teams as fabricators and both have made their mark on Delaware racing history. Today, Bobby and Beau spend their time fabricating and building some of the most impressive Street Rods in the country, continuing to show off their family's fabricating skills.

27

GARY TRICE

Since the 1950s, the Trice name has been involved in racing on the Delmarva Peninsula. Bill Trice and his brother Floyd were stock car pioneers during racing's infancy in the state of Delaware, winning the 1958 Sportsman Championship at Georgetown Speedway. The Trice brothers raced from the early 1950s until the '60s. When some area tracks closed down, the brothers retired. Bill's sons Gary and David Trice remember the impact of watching their dad and uncle race and work on cars during those early years.

> *Back then, they would race all over the place. I remember them towing the cars home and parking them in the front yard and working on them right in the yard. I remember Dad getting underneath an old GMC and pulling the base off the engine, changing the bearings and then going off to the next race. Those moments are what really got me and my brother David interested in racing. Over the years, he had a number of the area's top drivers run his car. Guys like J.R. Jones, Russell Townsend and Bob Maddux are the ones I remember most. From what my mom told me, Dad started out with a 1933 Chevrolet as his first race car, and that is where our car number 33 came from. Since the car was a '33 model, he just used that number, and it has been our number ever since.*

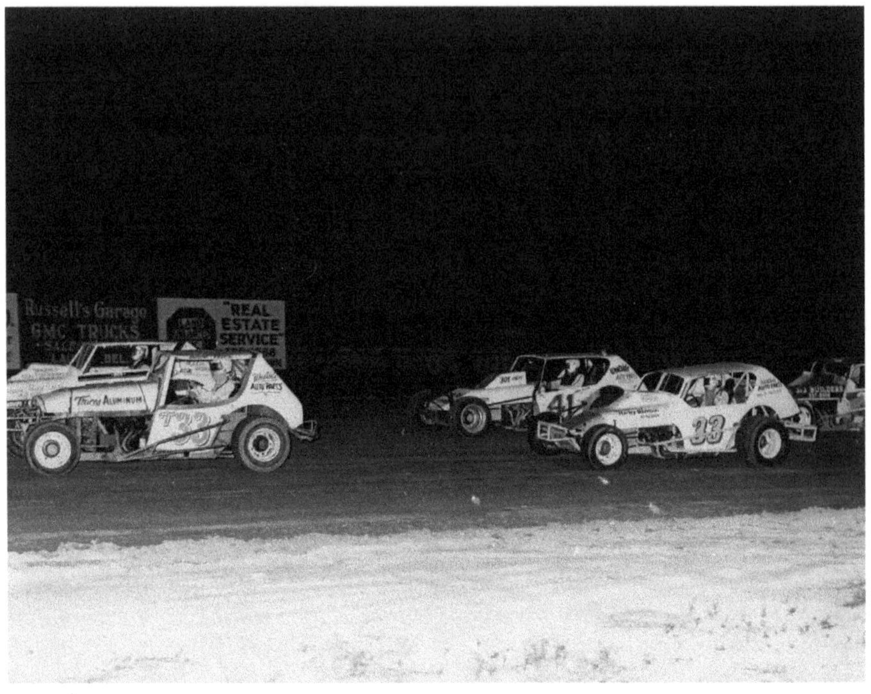

David Trice in the T33 leads brother Gary Trice in the no. 33 down the backstretch at Georgetown Speedway. *Courtesy of Don and Linda Allen, D&L Photos.*

Although the Trice family had been involved in racing, when Gary showed an interest in getting behind the wheel, his father was reluctant to jump back into the sport at first, as Gary explains.

> *When I turned eighteen and was a senior in high school, a friend of mine by the name of Kurt Kennedy and I decided we were going to go racing. We purchased a 1955 Chevrolet from Earnest Clark's Garage in Gumboro, Delaware. I think we paid one hundred bucks for the car. We had it up to a garage in Delmar and the guy started to put a roll cage in it and help us out. Well, my dad was not involved in racing at the time, and he did not want to get back into it again. About that time when we were doing the car on our own, my mom got mad at Dad for not helping us with the car. I guess she hounded him enough, and he started to help us. She loved racing just as much as us and was a track scorer for many years. We brought the car down to our house, and he started making the car safer. We worked right out in the yard, no*

garage or nothing. He put a safer roll cage in the car, and we started going racing, just the three of us, myself, Kurt Kennedy and Dad. Kurt and I took turns driving, alternating every other week. Kurt tore the car up every time he would get into it, and we would have to work on the car all week to get it running so I could race it. I never tore it up much, because I was so timid. After a frustrating race at Little Lincoln Speedway, Kurt quit driving, and that left just me and Dad fielding the car. We raced with limited success for a few years, but it was not until Uncle Floyd got us our first sponsorship from Westside Auto Parts owner Minus Givens in 1976 that things really started to click.

Indeed, 1976 was a big year for Gary. Winning two feature events at both US 13 Speedway and Georgetown Speedway gave the young racer newfound confidence in his abilities. Gary would also capture the coveted Delaware State Modified Champion title at the state fairgrounds in Harrington. Finally finding Victory Lane was a dream come true, but Gary was most proud of how they achieved the task.

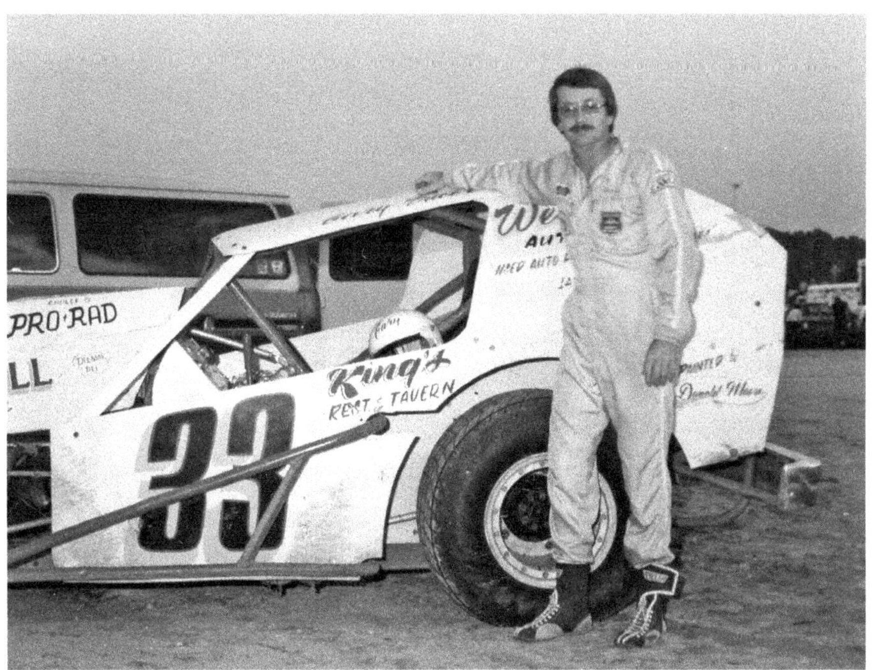

Gary Trice getting ready to pilot his own no. 33 Modified, sponsored by West Side Auto Parts. *Courtesy of Don and Linda Allen, D&L Photos.*

> *We won five features in 1976 in a car that Dad and I built out of pipe and two-by-four tubing in our shop. We were winning races in a car we built. Dad was a super smart guy and was the one who brought the alcohol carburetor down here to this area. He made it out of a standard Holly carburetor. Many of the other teams tried to buy that carburetor, but he never would sell it. If it was not for him, me or my brother David would have not had the success we had in racing. We continued racing and in 1977 won five more races along with our first championship. We ended up winning the Georgetown Speedway Modified Championship that year. We came back and repeated the following years as champion. Those were good years, and I can say my biggest wins came at that time. The two championships at Georgetown Speedway in 1977 and 1978, the two Delaware State Modified Championships at the State Fairgrounds and my 1977 Camp Barnes race win stand out as the biggest and most memorable wins of my career. The Camp Barnes race win was extra special to me, especially looking back years later, because after I quit driving in 1989, I had a driver named Deron Rust who drove for me for three years and he won the Camp Barnes race in 1994 in my car. Now my son, Brad Trice, is racing and he has won three Camp Barnes races, two in the Crate Modified class on one in the Big Block Modified class.*

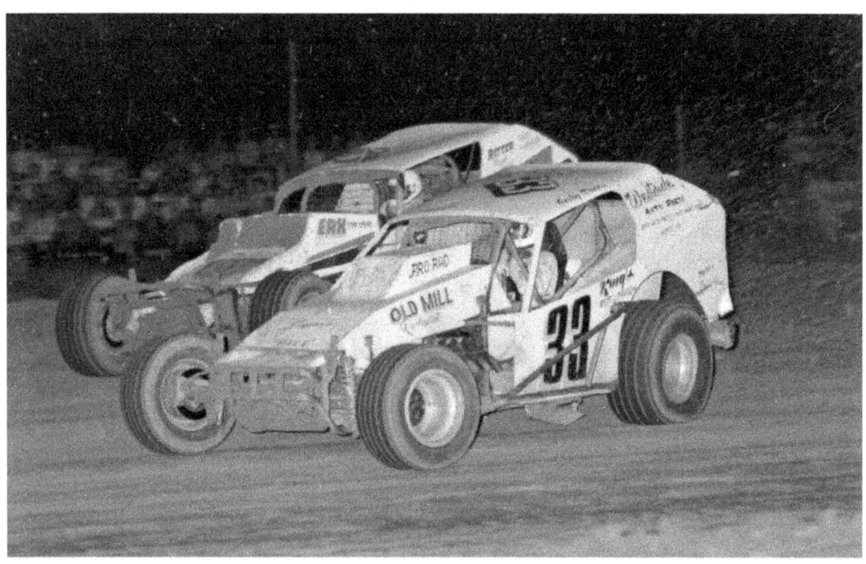

Gary Trice in the no. 33 drives under the no. 25 of Freddy Brightbill at US 13 Speedway during the 1983 race season. *Courtesy of Don and Linda Allen, D&L Photos.*

Travel to a race today in Delaware and you will see Gary's son Brad still carrying on the family tradition in the familiar no. 33 Big Block Modified. Since starting out racing Karts in the mid-nineties, Brad made his way up through the ranks racing Crate Modifieds and winning championships in the class before moving up into the Big Block Modified class. A skilled fabricator as well as a successful racer, Brad carries on the winning legacy of his dad and his grandfather, ensuring that the no. 33 and the Trice name will be seen around the track for some time to come.

28
BOB GEIGER

Perhaps one of the most beloved characters in racing history in and around Delaware is racer Bob Geiger and his no. 38 Late Model. As a young man, Bob was a champion roller-hockey player and speed skater. His no. 38 came from his jersey number in his hockey-playing days. Still going strong and racing today, Geiger has seemingly been involved in racing forever. Falling in love with racing as a boy, Geiger has seen many changes in his long career. Interestingly enough, his first race did not happen in the United States, but in Germany. Geiger explains how he got his love of racing and his first start.

> *My brother used to hang out with some racers from Salisbury. When there was talk of the Cathells building a dragstrip, I wanted to go see it so bad, but I was too young to hang out with the guys, so to speak, so they tried to make me stay home. But I got on my bicycle and rode on down to the track and actually beat my brother and his friends to the gate. I was right there when Charlie and Bill opened the gates for the first time. My dad had taken me to some stock car races in Pennsylvania before we moved down here to Delaware. We went to Hatfield and Langhorn Speedways, so I was a little bit familiar with stock car racing as a child. After a little bit of time, the Cathells built a Stock Car track next to the dragstrip at Delmar, and I started to go there as well. At that time, I was still pretty much just interested in drag racing. When I joined the army, I found a story in Stars and Stripes magazine about stock car racing in Germany, where I was*

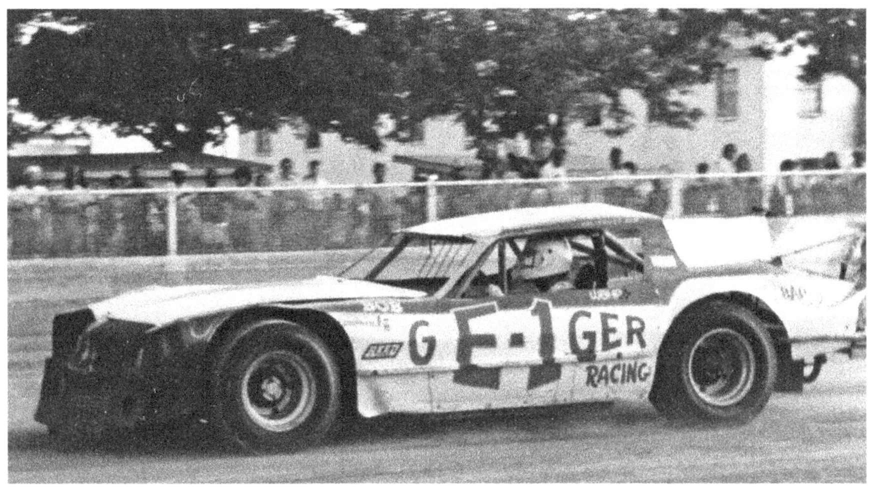

Late Model legend Bob Geiger makes the rounds at the 1980 Delaware State Fair. *Courtesy of Don and Linda* Allen, *D&L Photos.*

> *stationed at the time. Another fellow in one of the other companies beside us was kind of into racing as well, so we got permission from our battalion commander to work on some cars we had in the motor pool and use an army truck to take them up to another army base and race them. I won my first race in September of 1971 in Germany. Ironically, that same day in the USA, the first World 100 Late Model race was run. I always joke that I was in the wrong country to race that day.*

After returning to the States, Bob became a construction superintendent and continued his love for racing.

> *I started in the Six-Cylinder Hobby class for a year and then I raced six-cylinder Modifieds for a year. After they did away with that class, I moved into the Late Model division and have been there ever since. I used to go to Wharton and Bernard in Salisbury, Maryland, for parts. John Theofiles, who did a bunch of engines, was a big help at the beginning of my career. I had the most success in the E1 car. That car won the World 100 in 1979 with Larry Moore driving. I won a bunch of races at Georgetown with that car. I traveled around with Larry, racing the NDRA circuit that year. A funny story on how I got that car was that I was looking for a car and went over to Walt Breeding's shop and was talking with him about racing and looking for a new car. I was thumbing*

through some racing magazines when Walt jokingly said that the P1 car that Larry Moore won the World 100 was for sale. Walt did not know I knew Larry, so I said, "Well, that's the car I am going to go buy," and I walked out the door as they were laughing, because they thought I was joking. Well, a couple of days later, Larry Hill and Walt spotted me driving through Cambridge, Maryland, with that car on my trailer, and they called me as soon as I got home. They were both at my house in a matter of minutes to check that car out. It was a special car.

One of Bob's greatest racing accomplishments is his attendance at the Winter Nationals at East Bay Speedway in Florida. Bob lists qualifying for the A Main at East Bay as one of his greatest accomplishments. For forty years, thirty-eight of them consecutively, Bob has made the long tow down to the one-third-mile dirt oval to race with the nation's best Late Model drivers.

Mom and Dad were going to Homestead to camp in the wintertime. My brother was down there with them, and we both loved racing. He told me there was a stock car racetrack down there that raced cars just like we had. So I loaded up my Nova and went on down. It has changed so much over the years. It was just a single race back then, and now it's a whole weeklong event with hundreds of cars showing up.

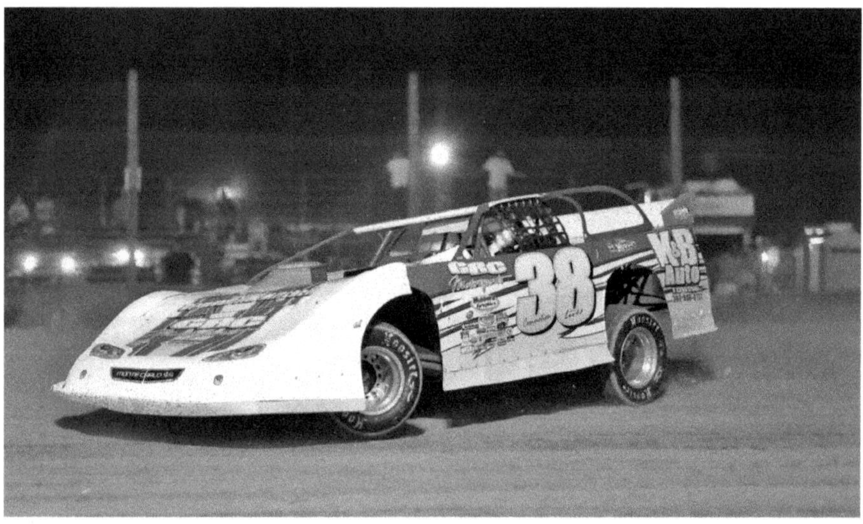

Still climbing behind the wheel after forty years, Bob Geiger slides his car into the corner at Delaware International Speedway. *Courtesy of Landstone Photography.*

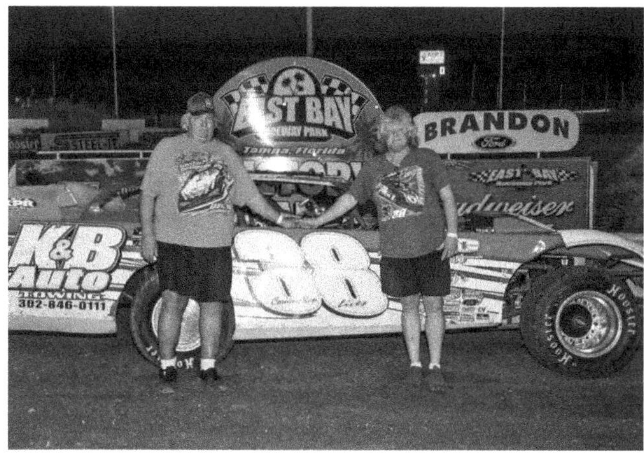

In 2019, East Bay Speedway in Florida honored Bob and Debbie Geiger for their thirty-eight consecutive years of participation at Speedweeks. *Courtesy of Bob and Debbie Geiger.*

The one constant over the years and the thousands of miles covered to go racing has been Bob's wife. Just as much a fixture at the track as Bob himself, Debbie Geiger has been along for the ride for some time. Bob talks a bit about her importance to the team and her love of racing.

> *Debbie loves racing as much as I do. She does all the work. She gets all the credit for what happens in the shop. I am not the winning car anymore, but I don't miss many laps. Nothing ever falls off or breaks. She is one hardworking girl. Debbie has been at it for over thirty-three years. I figure if she is good enough to work for Larry Moore and win the World 100, she is good enough to do it for me. We both have been all over the place racing and working on cars.*

Friends, family, race cars and having a good time are what it is all about for the Geigers. Probably no one in the pit area does more with less than Bob and Debbie Geiger. One thing is for sure, no matter what track you see the no. 38 Late Model pull into, you will see all the competitors eventually make it over to its pits to say hi to two of the nicest people you will ever meet in racing.

29
RON KEYS

Many people will remember the excitement created on the track in the 1980s by a shaggy, long-haired fifteen-year-old boy named Ron Keys. Ron and his dad, Earl Keys, certainly shook up the local race scene when they showed up to the track in their no. 39 Keys Trucking–sponsored Modified. Ron's age did not stop him from competing with some of the top talent of the era, and by the time he was seventeen, he had placed his Modified in Victory Lane, racing against some of the best drivers ever. Earl talks about how it all got started for the no. 39 team.

> *I loved racing and sponsored a figure-eight car at Dorsey Speedway. I said something to the driver one week about how I would like to own a Late Model race car. The next thing I knew, two weeks later, I owned a Late Model. I never drove any of those big cars; however, I did drive Mod Lites after Ron quit racing. I was strictly an owner during those early days. That car was a '67 or '68 Camaro. I would show up to the track sometimes with the car and try to find someone to drive it for me. For a while, Frankie Kerr drove it on Friday nights for me, and even Walt Breeding drove for me as well. That's what I did until Ron got old enough to drive. Ron got started at age thirteen, when he started driving a "slide for five" car. Not long after that, we moved up into the Street Stock class, and we had some success there. A few weeks after Ron's fifteenth birthday, I put him in Modified, and that's the class we raced until we quit many years later. During our time racing, we dabbled in Sprint Cars*

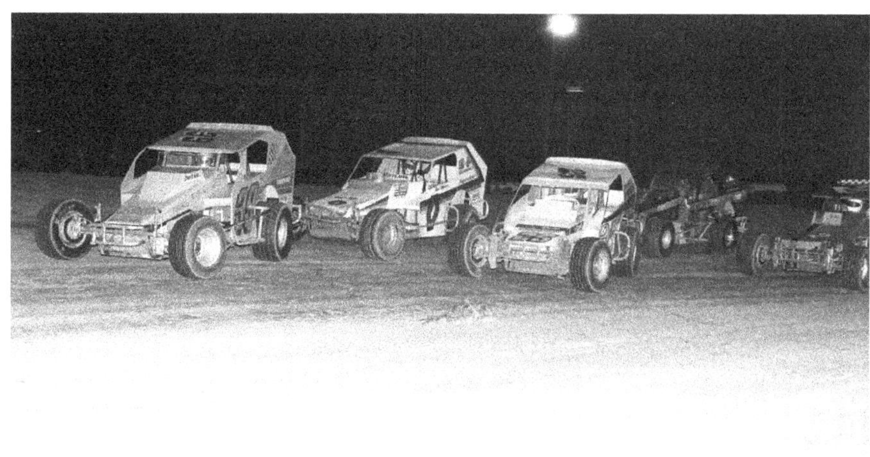

Ron Keys leads the pack during a feature event action in the late 1980s. *Courtesy of Don and Linda Allen, D&L Photos.*

> *for a few years, racing in the URC and in some 410 Sprint Car racing as well, but we ran the Modified at the same time, so we had two classes we were racing in for those years. We loved racing, so we didn't mind putting in the time needed to run multiple cars.*

Ron Keys won his first race at age seventeen and remembers racing during what many consider to be the golden age of Modified racing in Delaware, when competitors would travel to the state to run Georgetown Speedway on Friday night and then spend the night and run US 13 Speedway on Saturday night. The double-race weekends were a good deal for competitors like the Keys, who made the over two-hour tow down from their home in Oxford, Pennsylvania. When asked who was his toughest competitor, Ron had this to say about the drivers of that era.

> *It was so competitive at that time. It would be a long list if I was to tell you who was the toughest of that time. There were just so many. Bob Toreky, Harold Bunting, Walt Breeding were there every week and were always on top of their game. Guys like Richard Jarvis were just wide open all the*

time. I mean 100 percent every lap. You could not even take a breath or you would lose five positions. At the end of a feature, you would just be spent both physically and mentally.

When asked about his favorite win, Ron tells a story about respect on the track from a fellow competitor that made one win very special for him.

I would have to say my biggest win was at the only time we ran at Penn National Speedway. We won the Delmar race on Saturday night and then loaded up and headed to Penn National to race on Sunday. We won the heat race, the cash dash and the feature event. We were just on that weekend, but I have to say that the race that meant the most to me was a win I had at Georgetown Speedway. I won a feature at Georgetown after battling all race long with Harold Bunting. I was running up high on the cushion, and he tried everything to get by me, and I mean everything. He was all over me the entire race right up until the finish. We barely won, but it was a hard-fought victory. Harold was a man of few words, and I had the upmost respect for him. After the race, Harold walked over

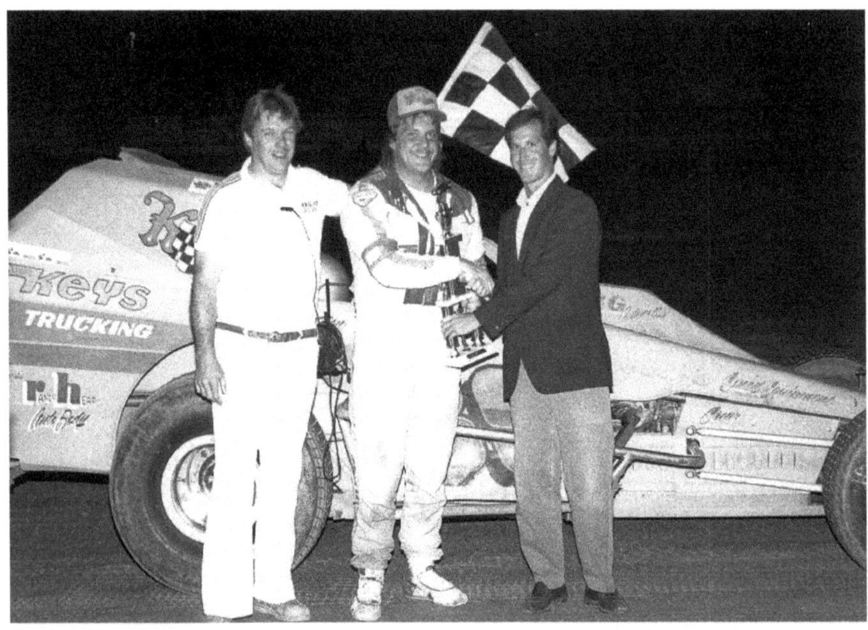

After climbing into a Modified at the age of fifteen, Ron Keys was quick to find success in the division. *Author's collection.*

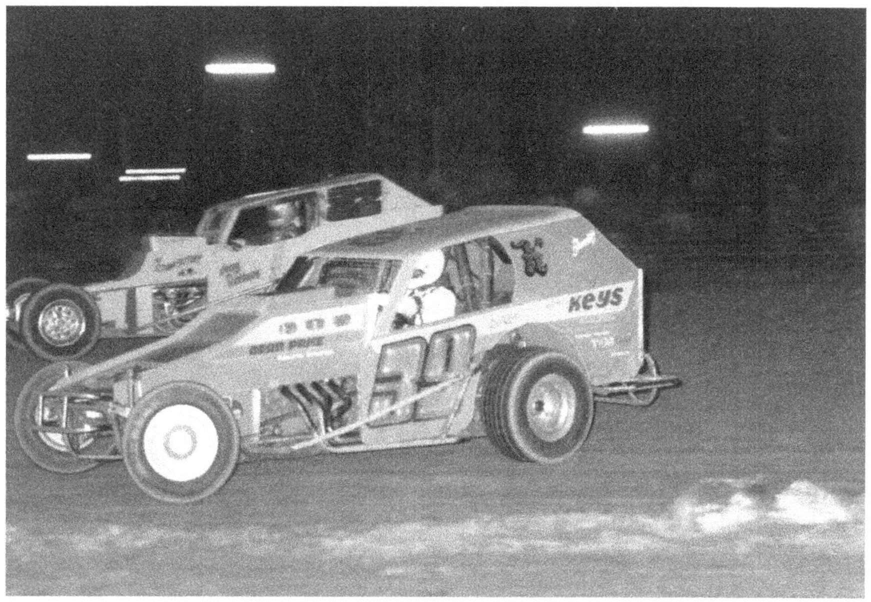

Ron Keys in the no. 39 on the gas and headed to the front under the no. 32 of Jerry Dickinson. *Courtesy of Don and Linda Allen, D&L Photos.*

> *to me and shook my hand and told me "That was a good race." I think that gesture really meant the world to me and remains one of my favorite memories of racing.*

Making the most of their time in Delaware, Ron Keys won feature events at Georgetown Speedway, Delaware International Speedway (formerly US 13 Speedway) and the Delaware State Fair Speedway in Harrington. Like so many other racers, the Keys raced as long as they enjoyed it and, when the time was right, gracefully walked away from the track as children were born and priorities in life changed. Both Ron Keys and father Earl Keys say they regret nothing about their time involved with the sport, and father and son enjoy where they are in life today, spending time with family and enjoying the next chapter of what is to come.

30

CHARLIE BROWN

For many years across the Delmarva Peninsula, if you went to a race, you often heard the voice of Charlie Brown coming out of the loudspeakers, calling the night's events and keeping fans informed on all the action going on at the track. Brown's familiar voice could be heard weekly at tracks like Georgetown Speedway and US 13 Speedway. When NASCAR comes to town for the Dover International Speedway races, it's Brown's voice you hear on the PA system, giving purpose and organization to what seems like a chaotic chorus of track events. From the time he was a child, Brown was a race fan. He got involved in racing through his father, Tom Brown.

> *My dad was a flagman who started when Melvin Joseph opened Georgetown Speedway. Dad also flagged the old Delmar Speedway owned by George Bowers when they were NASCAR sanctioned. He flagged at the Fairgrounds in Harrington and occasionally at Wilmington Speedway as well. So most weekends I was around his friends and people that just generally loved racing. Even AAA Racing Champion and Indianapolis 500 qualifier Bob Saul, who was a good friend of Dad's, would come by our house and hang out. We always had racing around us.*

The years of being around racing certainly had a profound impact on the young Charlie Brown. In the mid-1970s, Brown started a career as a school counselor. In his time off, he also soon found his way into the announcing booth, like some of the heroes he looked up to during his youth, and started following his passion for racing.

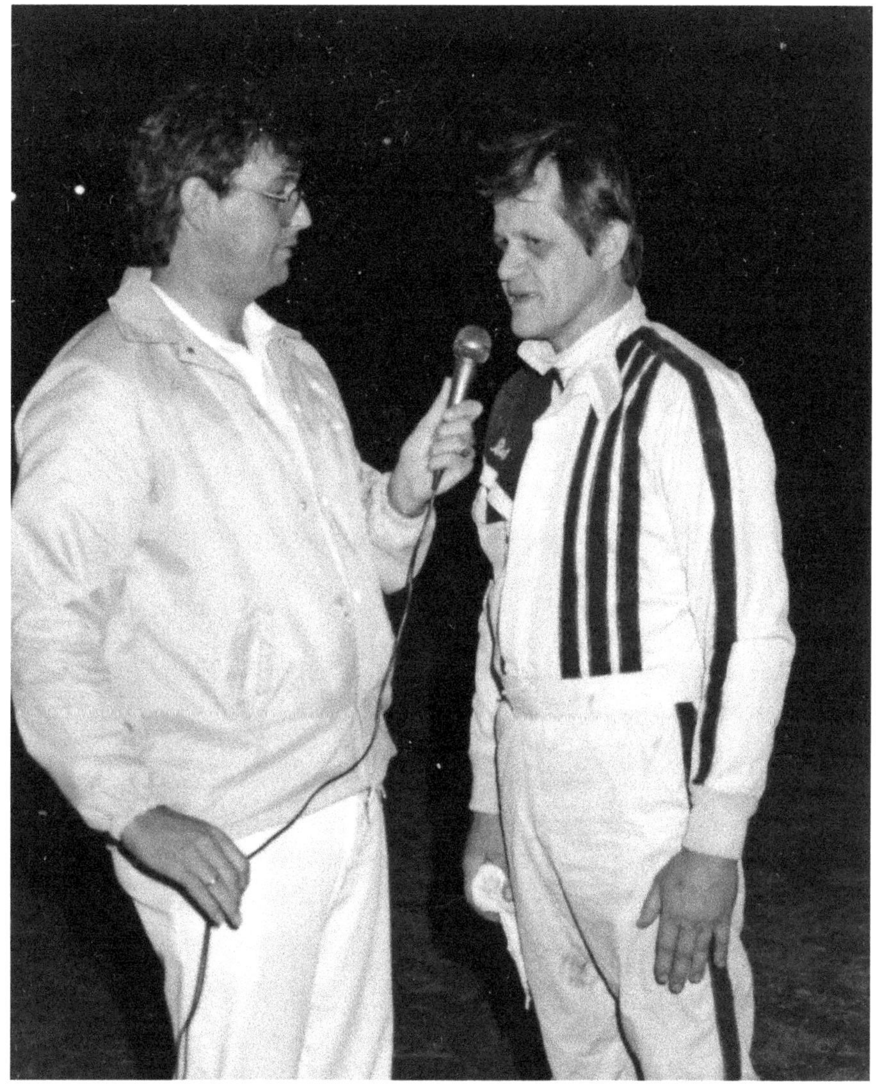

Charlie Brown (*left*) interviews winner Bob Toreky (*right*) at Georgetown Speedway in 1986. *Courtesy of Don and Linda Allen, D&L Photos.*

I grew up listening to a lot of racing on the radio. My heroes were guys like Warren Ruffner, who announced at Reading Speedway, Bill Singer, who announced at Flemington Speedway, and guys like Barney Hall, who were just on the radio all the time. Local broadcaster Bob McGinley from Georgetown, Delaware, was a good family friend who announced at

Georgetown Speedway. He became one of Motor Racing Network's (MRN) first broadcasters and was a big influence on me. I would have to say my biggest influence was Chris Economaki. I would listen to him announce the Indianapolis 500 on the radio before it was on TV all the time. I can't remember how old I was, but I remember realizing what Chris Economaki had to do was paint a picture of what was going on in the race. It was not like television, where you could just talk about anything and everything. He had to really describe in detail what he was seeing on the track, and he was just really excellent at doing that. It was around 1977 when I got my start announcing at the track, right around when Walt Breeding and Harold Wingate took over promoting Georgetown Speedway. It was just one of those things that kind of happened naturally. Walt Breeding had a guy announcing who was a radio disc jockey, and he could speak really well but did not know so much about racing. He just did not know the cars, drivers or any of their backgrounds. So after about two weeks, I walked up to Walt and I told him, "I have never announced before, but I think I could do better than the guy you have." I told him I would like to give it a try and if he didn't like me he would not have to pay me. He looked at me and said, "OK, you're on next week!" That is how I got started behind the microphone.

Honing his craft in those early days, Brown would soon also venture over to US 13 Speedway to announce for legendary promoters and track owners, the Cathell family. At one point, the busy Brown was announcing at both competing tracks.

Around 1988, I was announcing at Georgetown, US 13 Speedway and the Dragway at US 13. I was too busy! I had a way of overcommitting myself sometimes. Gerald Banks, who was a successful businessman and car owner, really pushed for Charlie Cathell to let me announce at US 13. I had been doing some writing for Charlie, and I was a corner flagman for a fall championship. I hated watching races from the stands. I always wanted to be involved somehow, so that's kind of how I worked my way in. Then, at some point, I was just down to announcing at US 13. I just cannot say enough kind words about Charlie Cathell and the whole Cathell family. They just became family to me and my family!

Although now retired from full-time announcing, Brown still finds time to fill in from time to time and continues to announce at both the spring

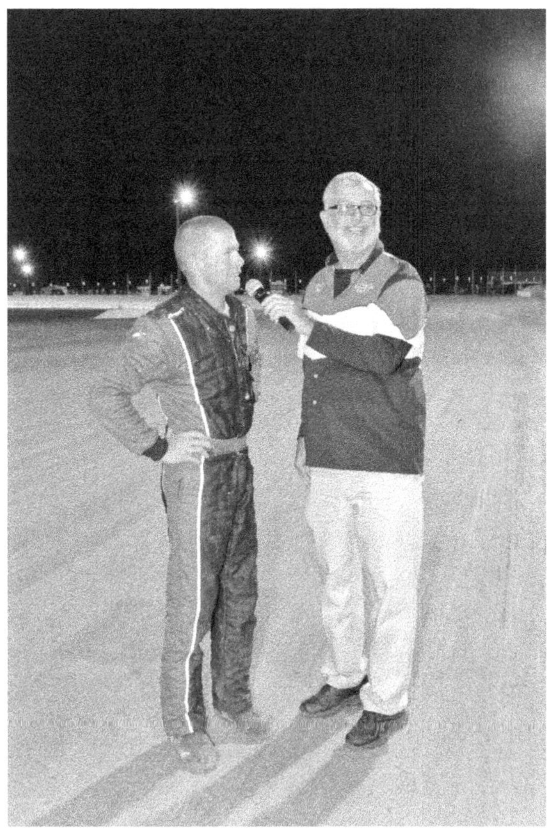

The voice of racing in Delaware, Charlie Brown (*right*) interviews driver Jamie Mills (*left*) at Delaware International Speedway. *Courtesy of Landstone Photography*.

and fall NASCAR Dover International Speedway races. Brown explains his beginnings at the NASCAR speedway.

> *Al Robinson, who was the PR chief for Dover Speedway, would come down to US 13 and watch the races. At the time, I had a racing radio show. So, he knew what I did. Alan Bestwick and Joe Moore were doing the track announcing at that time at Dover, but they were also working for MRN, so when they asked me to fill in for those guys when they had to go do their radio stuff, I said "Sure." So they put me in the booth, and as soon as those guys found out I could cover them and do the announcing, they stayed with the MRN broadcast and I took over the track announcing.*

One thing is for sure, if you attended a race in Delaware from the 1970s through 2017, you probably heard the smooth sound of Charlie Brown's voice coming over the loudspeakers, describing in great detail the night's action and keeping fans both new and old informed about what was going on. Like some of the great announcers at America's most famous and largest ballparks, Charlie Brown simply made the night's events at a track better and more entertaining for all who attended. For that, we the fans are deeply grateful.

31

LOU JOHNSON

Living in the shadow of Georgetown Speedway, Lou Johnson has just about seen and experienced it all at Delaware's local speedways. A multiple track champion at both Delaware International and Georgetown Speedways, Johnson is one of the area's most consistent and well-liked drivers. Now responsible for Georgetown Speedway's track preparations, Johnson has probably logged more laps around that speedway than anyone else, according to current promoter Brett Deyo. Working for the Delaware Department of Transportation, Johnson has always been familiar with heavy equipment. Add that to his decades-long driving career, and you have a racer who understands what it takes to make a track surface as perfect as possible. Johnson explains:

> *I have messed with dirt all my life, so I know what kind of moisture to put down on what kind of surface we have. I have seen Georgetown Speedway just as black and hard as the highway when one owner had it, and we used calcium. Then, when Tony Donofrio was running the track and the cars were running drag rubber tires, it would have a cushion about a foot and a half tall. With all the different types of clay that have been put on the track throughout the years, you always do what is best for the track at that given time. Currently, I wet the top and keep the track kind of greasy so as the track sees laps during the night, it really comes together for feature time.*

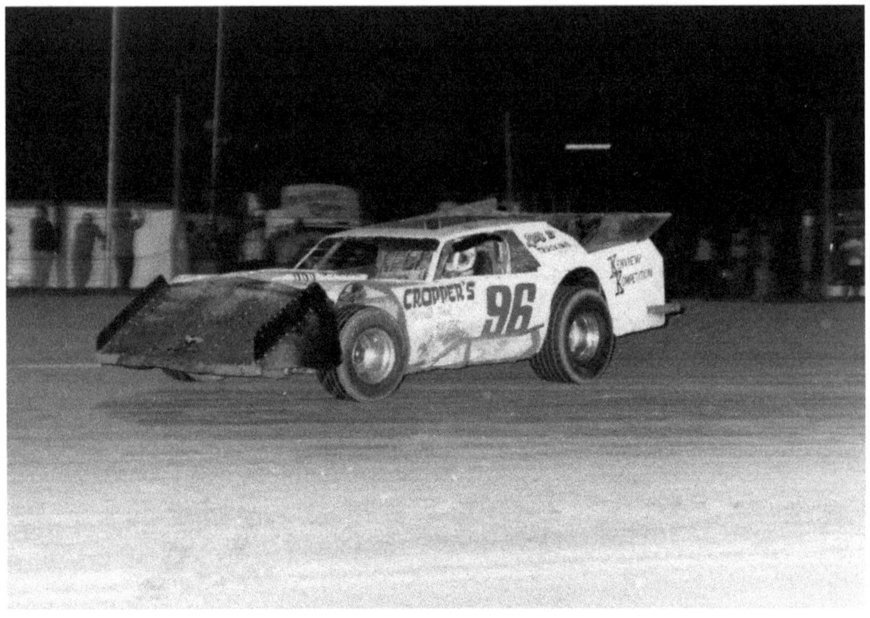

During the wedge-style era of Late Model racing Lou Johnson was a weekly threat for the win. *Courtesy of Don and Linda Allen, D&L Photos.*

Known for being easy on equipment and winning championships, Johnson's driving style was as smooth and consistent as any racer in Delaware's history.

> *My theory was if my car was not brought in on a hook at the end of the night, I was going to make some money. I never ran for a championship unless it got down to the last couple races, and then I would start to battle really hard. But I never worried about the championships at all. They just automatically come. My thing is I am going to be there every week and I wanted to finish every race. One year at Delaware International Speedway, I went a year and a half and always finished on the lead lap. I never lost a lap in that time during a qualifier, heat race or feature.*

Although known for his reliability and consistent high-place finishes, luck was not always on Johnson's side.

> *There were lots of times I would be leading on the last lap and break, run out of fuel or cut a tire. At one race, my wife said jokingly earlier in the*

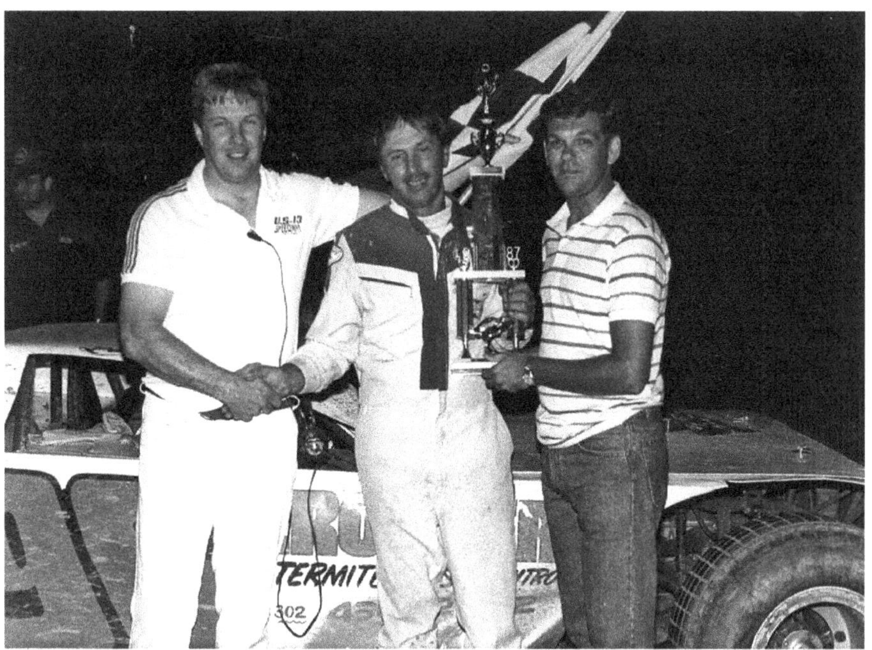

Lou Johnson (*center*) stands in Victory Lane with flagman Bruce Webb (*left*) and policeman and state representative Biff Lee (*right*) in 1987. *Author's collection.*

night, "Why don't you just wait until the last lap to take the lead," since I was having such bad luck while leading the races. So, I thought, "Well, OK!" So, I was running second in the feature to Hal Browning, and I was thinking about what Joyce said, so I just sat behind him until there was one to go. We went down the backstretch, and when I tried to pass him, we got together and I got turned into the wall and the throttle stuck and it broke the brake line. I had no brakes and no throttle. I was trying to reach for the switch to shut the car down, but there was no way. The hit broke the tie rods, so I could not steer the car as well. That car went off of turn three and soared over the drop and went through the fence and struck the toilet on the other side. Half of the car was hung on the fence and teeter-tottering back and forth over the ledge. I was so stunned, I climbed out of the car and fell right to the bottom of that huge ledge back there. That was my first Late Model I bought off of Walt Breeding. When I saw Joyce after the wreck that night, she said jokingly, "Well, I didn't mean for things to happen that way." I told her she didn't have to worry about that again, because I was never going to wait until the last lap to pass anyone again. We raced clean back then, and that wreck was one of them racing deals.

Racing for over forty-five years, Johnson would do it all over again.

> *I was very fortunate and never got hurt. I flipped upside down one time I can remember, and the car landed on its wheels and I finished the race. That was in the Everett Messick–owned Modified. That was the most ill-handling car I ever drove. The shock tower clipped a tire and flipped me end over end and around. It landed right on its wheels and knocked the front and back bumpers off the car. The bumpers were made of aluminum, which I did not know at the time. The wrecker guys told me the tires were still up and I could drive it to the pits. I thought, "Well, if I can drive it to the pits I can finish this race," so that's what I did. When I got in the pits, they told me I knocked all four shocks off the car, but it had torsion bars anyway. After that, the car didn't work that bad, and I ended up getting second in the feature with the same car. They wired the bumpers on so we could start.*

Johnson looks back fondly over those golden years of racing on the Delmarva Peninsula. The five-time track champion at Delaware International Speedway and six-time track champion at Georgetown Speedway is quick to tell you he never really stopped racing or retired. Although Johnson stays

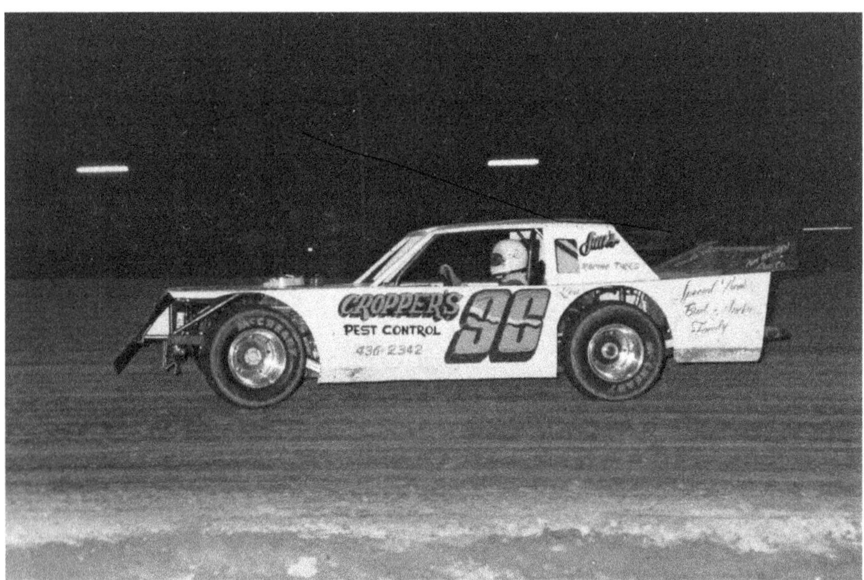

Lou Johnson was a five-time track champion at Delaware International Speedway and a six-time track champion at Georgetown Speedway. *Courtesy of Don and Linda Allen, D&L Photos.*

busy keeping the clay at Georgetown Speedway perfectly groomed, don't be surprised if you see the familiar no. 96 show up in some form at the track sometime in the future. Lou Johnson just might decide to abandon the grader for a night and hop back in something faster to make a few laps and remind us all of the champion racer he is and always will be.

32
CURT MICHAEL

The state of Delaware has had its fair share of winning Modified and Late Model racers. While the Modified and Late Model classes of race cars dominate the local weekly racing scene, every fan loves when the winged Sprint Cars of the United Racing Club (URC) come into town for a special show. One of the most successful racers in the history of the URC is Ocean View, Delaware's Curt Michael. Michael is not only one of the winningest drivers in the long history of the URC, but he also currently holds the record for most championships, with an impressive total of ten URC titles. Not bad for a kid from Pennsylvania who got his start racing Quarter Midgets and Micro Sprints.

> *I grew up in Allentown, Pennsylvania, where my older brothers were both involved in racing. Chris would later go on to race Modifieds at Nazareth Speedway, and Sean would go on to be successful in the URC, winning many races and two URC championships. After turning the wrenches for my brother at Linda's Speedway for some time, I was finally able to jump in a Micro Sprint and give it a try. I was hooked instantly! We ran those cars from 1991 through 1994, winning a championship at Linda's Speedway in 1993. It was during this same time our family made the move to Ocean View, Delaware, after coming down to the area for many years. In 1995, we decided it was time to move up to a full-size Sprint Car. The timing was good, because Georgetown Speedway was running a series of six Sprint Car races that year. We built a 358 Sprint Car and won four out of six races at Georgetown Speedway in our first year running.*

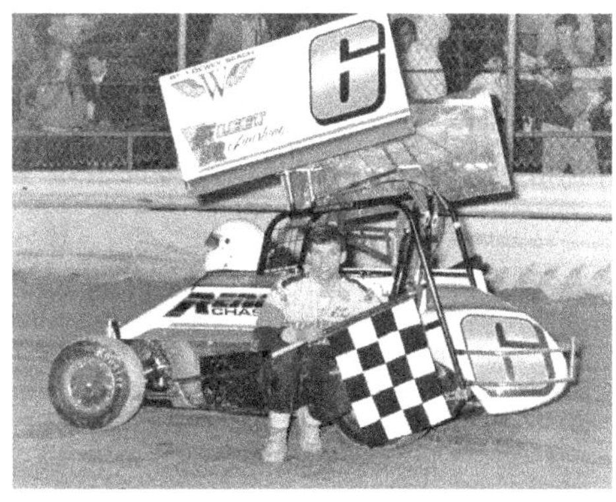

Before jumping in a full-size Sprint Car, Curt Michael was a champion Micro Sprint driver. *Courtesy of Curt Michael.*

After experiencing success in their first year of running full-size Sprint Cars, Curt and his dad, Al, made the jump to racing with the URC in 1996 using a 360-cubic-inch engine from Mike Bostic. Michael would finish tenth in points his first year racing with the URC and win his first race. Ironically, Michael's first win would come at what would be the last URC race at the famed Harrington Raceway at the Delaware State Fairgrounds. With such a long history of hosting open-wheel racing, it was fitting that a Delawarean should win the last open-wheel Sprint Car race at the speedway. After a successful first year in the URC, Michael set his sights on winning more races and even championships.

> *My dad and I had a five-year plan to get a ride in the URC. So, that first year, it was a family-run deal, and then when Mike Bostic came into the picture, things really started to progress. In 1997, we won three races and finished third in the URC Championship while my brother Sean won the championship that year. I knew we could win a championship. That is the kind of driver I am. I am consistent and easy on equipment. If I have a fourth-place car, most likely we are going to finish in fourth place. I never saw the need to take an unnecessary risk and tear a car up for a spot we just could not obtain. My style lends itself to championships. It's a lot easier to race the next week when you don't tear equipment up, and you just don't break down as much when you are building new cars every other week.*

Michael's smooth style and consistency paid off in 1998, when he and the Mike Bostic team won the URC Championship in Curt's signature style. Sprint Car legends Kramer Williamson and Greg Coverdale won a total of fourteen races between them, and Michael won three. But it was Michael's consistency week in and week out that would give him the edge in his first

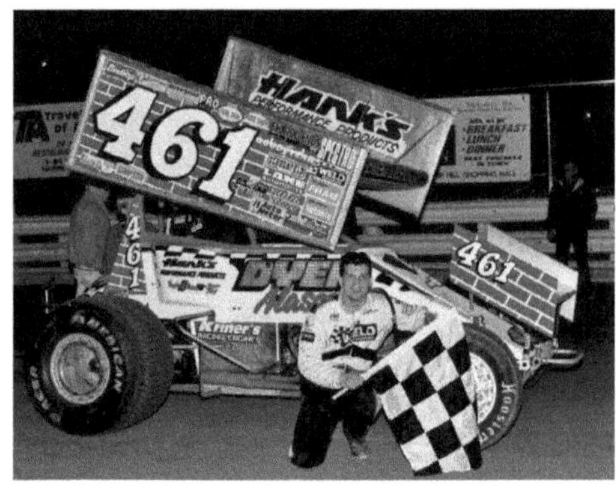

Curt Michael has driven for some of the best Sprint Car teams around. Here he is in Victory Lane with the Walt Dyer–owned no. 461 "Brickmobile" Sprint Car. *Courtesy of Curt Michael.*

of many championships. The next few years would see Michael running many 410 Sprint Car shows in the central Pennsylvania area for car owners such as Mike Bostic, Bill Tanger and Walt Dyer. Winning features at Lincoln Speedway and Williams Grove Speedway were highlights of his time in the powerful 410 Sprint Cars. Curt soon returned to chase more championships in the URC series, but in 2002, while driving for Pat Palladino, disaster struck at Delaware International Speedway when Michael's car hit the tire of another car, flipping violently. Michael's back was broken in the process. While Michael would make a full recovery, it would take him away from racing for nine long months. During that time, he married his longtime girlfriend, Jennifer, who just happens to be a former Ms. Motorsports. Curt remembers his return to racing after the injury.

> *When I got back in the car for the first time after that accident, it was tough. I mean, I was all over the place, and I just had to get my mind right. Everyone thought I was spooked. Even my wife turned to the owner and said, "Great! He has turned into a wuss!" During that time, I just remember what my older brother told me about Sprint Cars and how they were designed to go fast, and the faster you drove them the easier they were to handle. So, after a conversation with myself, I hit the gas and eventually found my stride again. We won four races that year. Two were at Delaware International, where I got hurt. I was really happy to win there and get that monkey off my back.*

In 2004, Michael went on a five-year tear, winning five championships in a row for three different car owners, a feat never before done in URC history and one likely not to be repeated. In 2008, Michael started driving for owner Bill Gallagher, for whom he still drives today. Between 2008 and

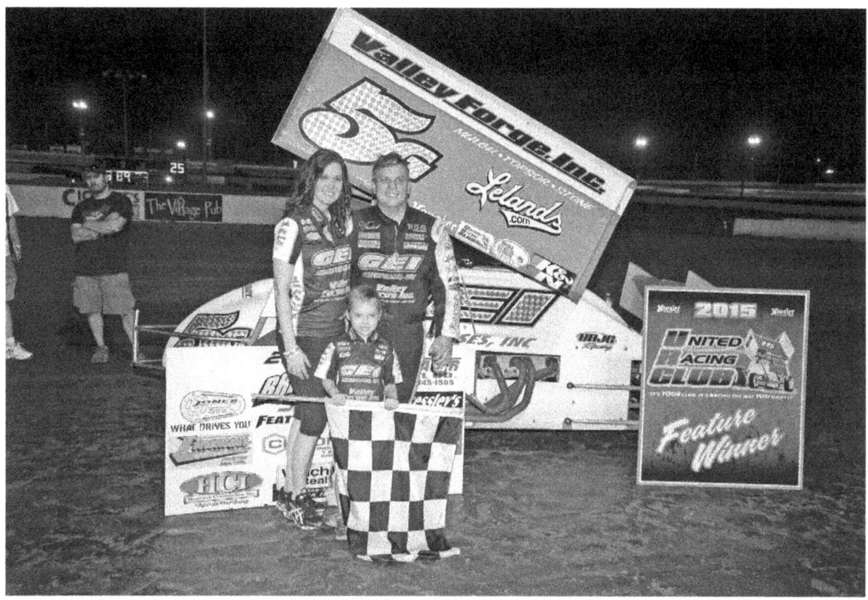

Ten-time United Racing Club champion Curt Michael in Victory Lane with his wife, Jenn, and daughter, Madison. *Courtesy of Rick Sweeten Images.*

2018, the two have added four additional URC Championships to Michael's impressive number of ten total URC Championships. Present-day Michael continues to race in the URC and tends to his busy graphics business. Racing is a full-time occupation for the Michael family, so it should not be a surprise that Curt and Jennifer's daughter Madison is now racing Quarter Midgets.

> *She is really good at it. Madison took right to it. She has already flipped it once, but she got right back in and finished the race. Within a few weeks, she was right back up front. We are really proud of her, and it has been an awesome experience getting to watch her progress.*

For the Michael family, racing is life. Curt continues to chase wins and championships. With the youngest member of the family, Madison, now winning races, it looks like the racing gene has been passed down to the next generation and that the Michael name will be involved in Sprint Car racing for some time to come.

33

RICKY ELLIOTT

One of the most successful drivers to come out of the First State is Seaford, Delaware's Ricky Elliott. A winner and champion in both Modifieds and Late Models, Elliott has mastered just about every class of racing popular on the Eastern Shore. Elliott got his start like most racers, cutting his teeth at various Karting tracks in the area, sharing his ride with his dad.

> *We started in 1980, when I was nine. Dad and I actually raced in Laurel on a track in between Craig Littleton's two chicken houses. It was actually kind of funny that we were both trying to race the same go-kart. My dad raced the heavy class, and I raced the light. Adding weight to the kart for me was no problem, but the difference in height was. We would have to modify the kart between the races so I could reach the pedals. It worked for a while, but eventually I became the sole driver and Dad turned the wrenches.*

Elliott would eventually reach the pinnacle of Kart racing by winning 135 races and the 1986 Regional and National Gold Cup championships. After reaching the top of the Karting mountain, Elliott was ready to move on to new challenges and set his eyes on running Big Block Modifieds. Not everyone bought into Elliott's enthusiasm to move up right away, including one of his biggest fans, his dad. "I was racing Karts in 1987 and I just lost my drive and was ready to move on. My dad was not ready to move on, but I was."

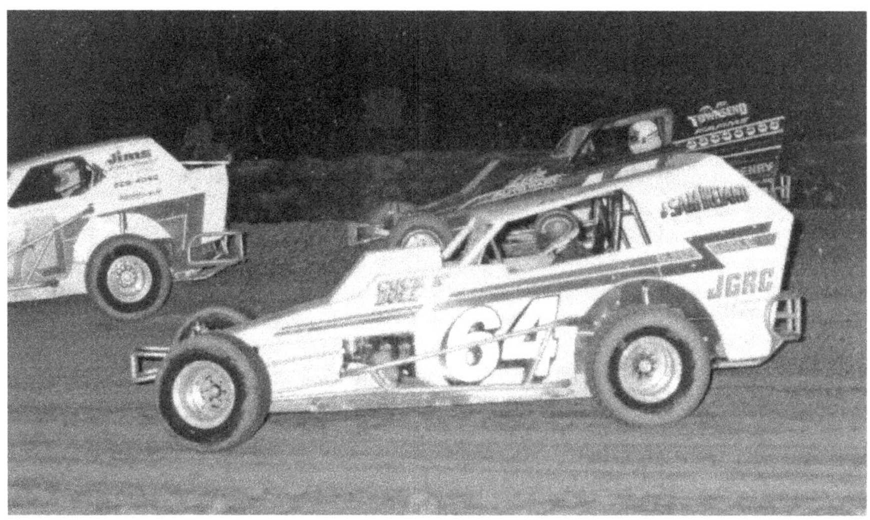

Ricky Elliott pilots his Olsen Eagle around Delaware International Speedway during his rookie year of racing. *Courtesy of Don and Linda Allen, D&L Photos.*

Ricky's dad explains:

> *Everything we ever did in Karting up to that point we had to pay for all of it and I mean all of it, the travel expenses and all. As soon as Ricky won the national championship, a company called Competition Karting picked him up and set us up with a brand-new kart, brand-new tires, brand-new motors, everything! Now that we have a great sponsor and we are getting stuff for free, he wants to quit!*

The lure of a great sponsor was not enough to keep Elliott in Karting, and although he did not have a concrete plan in place, he knew it was time to move up. Racing is often about sacrifice and taking chances. Moving up from Karts to a Modified certainly was a big jump in more ways than one for Elliott.

> *Ed Brown had a brand-new Olsen car he bought in 1986, and he only ran like five races with it, and I went over and looked at it, went to the bank and borrowed three thousand dollars to buy this rolling chassis without a motor. I had to go get a trailer. I brought that car home, and when my dad came home, he saw the car sitting in the driveway and said, "Who's car is that?" I said it was mine and told him I was going race that car, and Dad*

> *finally figured out I was very serious about the whole deal, and he started selling off all the Karting stuff. After I paid the chassis off myself, a bunch of guys and I went to the bank again and borrowed three thousand dollars between the four of us. We used that money to buy a used steel-headed motor from Bucky Weber.*

The big chance paid off in Ricky's first full year of racing, when he won the Diamond State 50. In the following years, Elliott would drive for some of the biggest owners in Modified racing, starting with the legendary no. 30 Mills Brothers Blue Hen Racing Team, winning eleven races and the Georgetown Speedway Championship in 1988–89. In his next season of competition, Elliott piloted the no. 19D Modified of Steve Dale and won twenty-five feature events as well as the Delaware International Speedway and Georgetown Speedway Championships. While racing for the team for only one year, Elliott credits his time with the no. 19D team and owner Steve Dale as one of his biggest educational experiences in racing. "It was probably the most growing up learning experience I had in a short period of time. I went from Karts to winning championships in Big Block Modified and dealing with all these different personalities in a very short time."

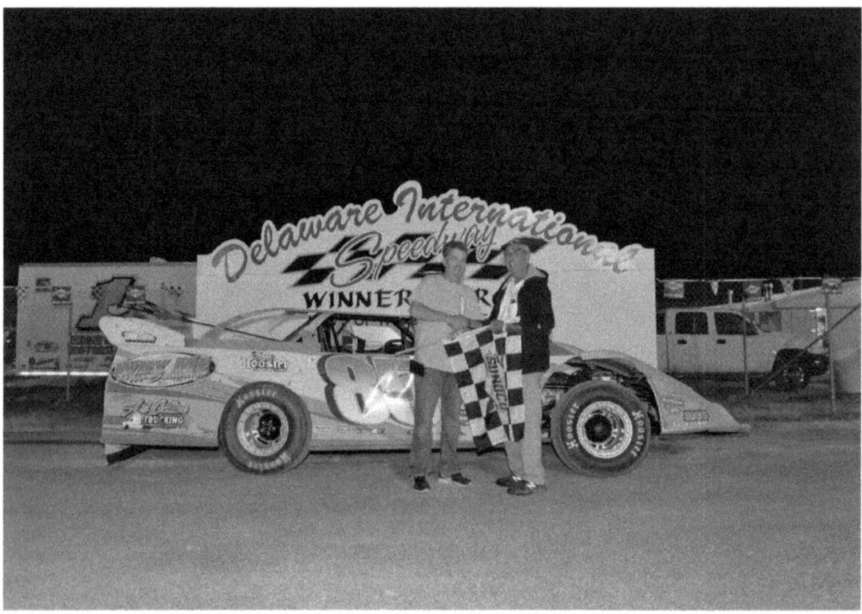

Ricky Elliott (*left*) gets congratulated by track owner/promoter Charlie Cathell (*right*) after yet another Late Model win. *Courtesy of Landstone Photography.*

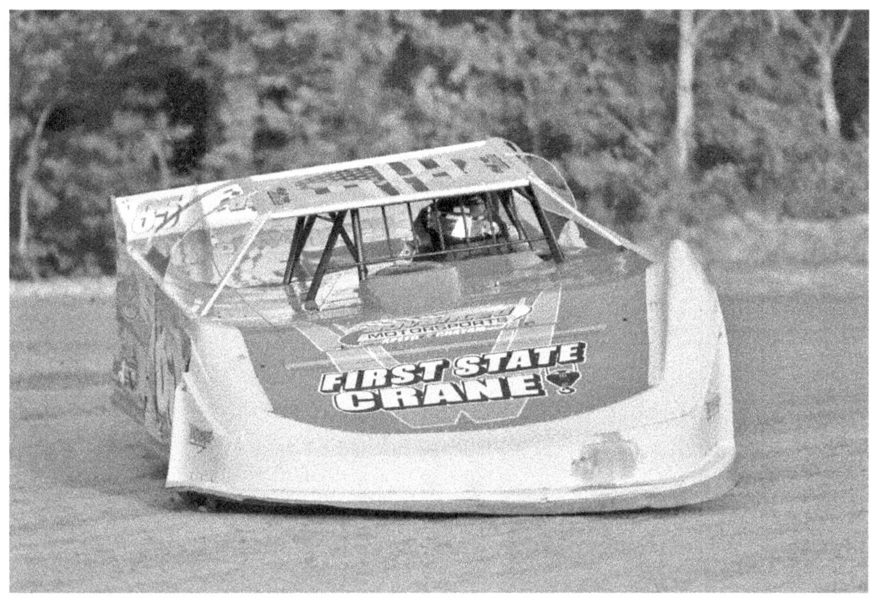

Ricky Elliott announced his retirement from racing at the end of the 2018 season after a winning career that spanned decades. *Courtesy of Landstone Photography.*

After splitting with the no. 19D team, Elliott would again land one of the top rides in the sport, piloting the no. 0 Overhead Door Big Block Modified. With a new team, the results were the same. During the 1991–92, season, Elliott again won over twenty-five races and championships at Delaware International and Georgetown Speedways. During his success at local tracks, Ricky also ventured out of the area and had equal success on the road. One of his biggest career wins came in a Modified at the dirt track at Charlotte Motor Speedway in 2004.

After spending most of his career in Modifieds, Elliott surprised many when he made the switch to racing Late Models. Although these were much different cars than the Modifieds, the results were more of the same. Elliott even started running with the World of Outlaws for owner Butch Warrington.

> *Butch just called me up and said, "Hey, I am going to go World of Outlaw Late Model racing. You want to drive?" And that was exactly how that happened. It was nice to travel around and race with the Outlaws and race a Late Model. I had been racing a Modified locally for so many years, and people would tell you not to run with this guy or do not hang around this*

guy because he is a jerk. It was refreshing to form your own opinion on everyone you raced with, because you did not know anyone and you formed your own opinion by being around them at the track. Instead of people not liking someone they don't know or talking about them, it was a nice change, because I had no one clouding my judgement of someone else.

Elliott's change to Late Models has produced many wins and championships. His Modified and Late Model championships, numbering in the double digits at both Georgetown and Delaware International Speedways, represent only a small portion of his winning career statistics. For many years, Elliott traveled outlaw style to hand-picked races all over the country, leaving him unable to compete for a championship at home while racking up wins on the road. One would need a larger book than this one to include his impressive list of wins and championships. Unafraid to race with the nation's best, Elliott became a popular driver up and down the Eastern Seaboard. Today, you can still find Elliott running his Advanced Motorsports shop in Seaford, Delaware. At the end of the 2018 season, he made the decision to retire from racing and pursue some lifelong bucket list items that he and his wife were simply not able to do while competing full time in racing. Ricky Elliott ended his career on his terms, winning the 2018 Delaware International Speedway Track Championship before stepping away from driving. He will be forever remembered as a winner, a champion and one of the best drivers to come out of the First State of Delaware.

34

BRETT DEYO

As one of the busiest guys in racing, promoter and Delaware resident Brett Deyo has revitalized racing not only at Georgetown Speedway but also up and down the East Coast. Deyo has become one of the most successful and sought-after promoters in the nation, as his races attract the sport's top drivers and are attended by thousands of enthusiastic fans. Known for well-organized shows that run on time, Deyo has recently moved to Delaware to be closer to one of his favorite tracks, Georgetown Speedway. Although a Delaware resident now, Deyo got his start attending the Modified races at New York's Orange County Speedway and Accord Speedway.

> *I grew up going to Orange County Speedway and sitting in the stands with my dad. That's what we did every week. Racing was probably the only thing that kept me getting good grades in school, because I always had to have a good report card to go to the races. In school, I always enjoyed writing, and in 1998, I was able to apply that to my love of racing. A paved track near us called Bethel Motor Speedway had reopened, and they just were not getting any press in any of the racing publications. Some friends of ours that raced there, John and Jeff Hager, said, "Why don't you call Area Auto Racing News (AARN) and give the writing deal a try." I was like fifteen or sixteen at the time and was doing a lot of writing for the school paper. So, I called Area Auto Racing News and ended up getting hooked up with Kevin Kovac, and he set me up to start covering the races in 1998. Then, in 1999, I started at*

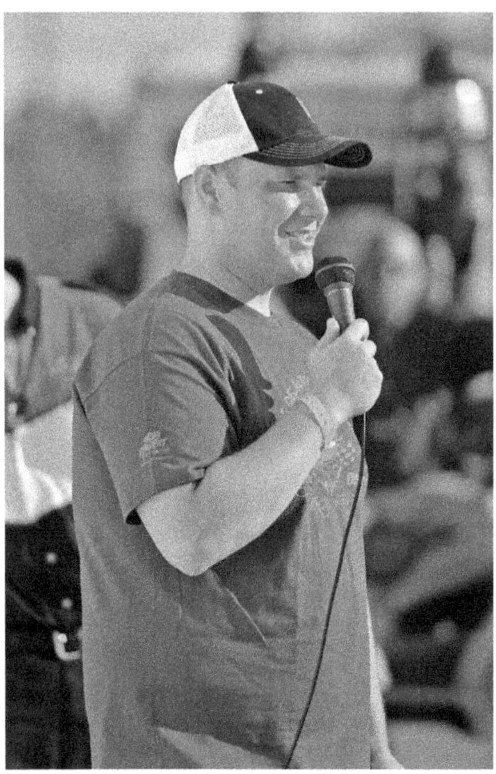

The arrival of promoter Brett Deyo at Georgetown Speedway has ushered in a new era of racing in Delaware. *Courtesy of Rick Sweeten Images.*

> *Accord Speedway, because they needed someone to cover their results, and it just kind of grew from there. I started to do public relations and some announcing at Orange County and Accord Speedways. So, my first job out of college in 2006 was working for Lenny Sammons editing for Area Auto Racing News, and that helped me really get hooked up with all the racetracks, which was a huge step towards promoting races.*

Throughout his time in high school and college, Deyo paid close attention to all the aspects of the racing industry, learning everything he could. Soon, he tried his hand at race promotion, using those years of experience working at the speedways and applying that knowledge to create a better racing experience. Promoters always take big risks, and perhaps there was no bigger risk for Deyo than the first race he promoted.

> *My first race was 2006 at Afton Speedway. That was the first Short Track Super Nationals. My crazy idea was that I was going to have a race on the same day as Super Dirt Week, and everybody thought I was insane. My*

thought was that there were so many race teams who just could not afford to go to Super Dirt Week, and at that time, it really just took some special equipment to run the big mile at Syracuse. A lot of people could just not afford to make that race. So, I really wanted to create a true workingman's race, and we ended up registering 56 Modifieds and 220 total cars. That race was a huge success, and I really did not have the money to do it. I only had $220 in my checking account. It was a huge gamble, and it had to work, or we were in trouble. The weather cooperated, we had two nice days of racing, and we made money, and that is what got us started. Then I started doing some promotions at different tracks, like Five Mile Point and Penn-Can. In 2013, I decided I was going to do promoting full-time. In 2014, we put the Short Track Super Series together, because I had so many tracks wanting to do something, so it just made sense to pull all of it together with a point fund. It just grew and grew. One race turned into five, five into ten, and then we started the series in 2014, and that was also the year we had our first race at Georgetown Speedway.

During years of covering the races in Delaware, Deyo began to form relationships that would become the catalyst for his eventual promotion of the speedway.

I really like Delaware. I have always enjoyed coming to the area. As I was working for AARN, I started to cover more and more of the racing at Delaware International Speedway, and I started to make friends with the racers and promoter Charlie Cathell. So, in 2011 and 2012, I would come to Delaware every other weekend and make it like a mini-vacation for me and my wife as I covered the races. Then, in 2014, Eric Kormann, who was racing a Big Block at Georgetown Speedway, came to me and said, "Why don't you try to do a race here at Georgetown?" He said he would do it with me because he knew the people over there, so we set up a meeting on a Friday night to discuss the possibility of having a race there. The place was struggling a bit, but you could just see the place had so much potential. So, we put that first Beach Blast race together, and it just blew everything out of the water that we could ever imagine. I think we had forty-eight Modifieds and a ton of Sportsman cars as well. The crowd was great and just super into the racing. But, the true miracle of that night was that nothing went wrong. As I got to be the promoter of Georgetown, I got to see all the things that had not been updated in years, so it was really a miracle

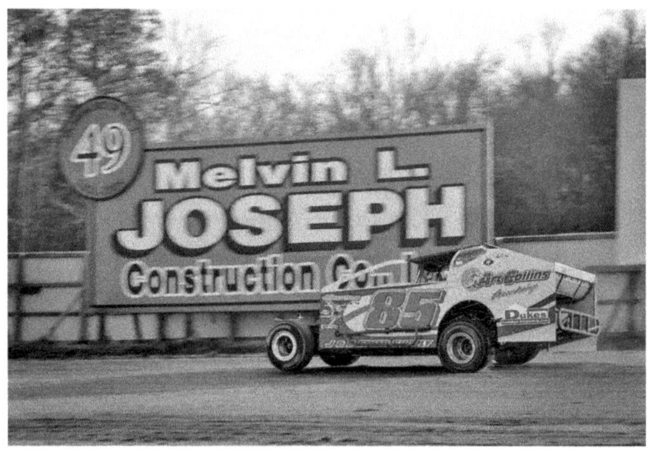

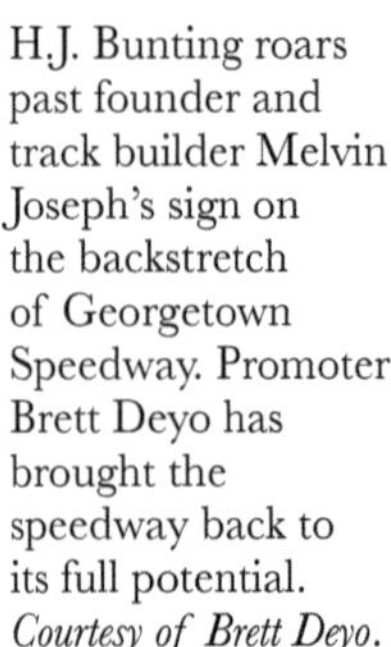
H.J. Bunting roars past founder and track builder Melvin Joseph's sign on the backstretch of Georgetown Speedway. Promoter Brett Deyo has brought the speedway back to its full potential. *Courtesy of Brett Deyo.*

> *that whole night went off without something going wrong, like the lights going off. It was almost like it was just meant to be! We went back the following year for a race in 2015, and in October of that year, we signed to take the track over. After seeing the support that Delaware gave the track, I just felt like it could be a great special events track.*

Some promoters are known for their cutthroat ways, but Deyo carries a reputation of professionalism and respect that is gained by his obvious love for the sport. Deyo's character can be seen in the way he approached the promotion of Georgetown Speedway.

> *I went to Charlie Cathell* [promoter and owner of Delaware International Speedway] *right up front before I signed any paperwork, because I have always gotten along really well with him and have a lot of respect for him. I said, "Listen, I am thinking about taking over Georgetown, but I am not going to do it as a means to hurt Delaware International Speedway." I told him that if we put our heads together we could both benefit. Nobody told me that was going to work out. Everybody said things like "That will never work out," but I am proud to say to this day, we still spend a lot of time together and are still good friends. I have always said Delaware International Speedway is the weekly track for racing in Delaware, so we need to support it. Georgetown is a special events track, and we can do a lot of cool things because we do not race every week, but we need to support Delaware International Speedway as well, and that relationship has made racing in Delaware stronger overall.*

Today, the busy Deyo continues to operate Georgetown Speedway as well as his traveling Short Track Super Series, running well-organized events and entertaining thousands of race fans yearly. Delaware is fortunate to still have two dirt tracks within a short distance of each other, both still operating and carrying on the strong heritage of our racing history. Brett Deyo's leadership and management style have been crucial for dirt track racing's resurgence not only in Delaware but also up and down the Atlantic Seaboard. His love of racing is obvious, and his passion will carry the sport into the future with unparalleled levels of success.

BIBLIOGRAPHY

Books

Culver, Chad Wayne. *Delaware Auto Racing*. Charleston, SC: Arcadia Publishing, 2012.

———. *Dover International Speedway: The Monster Mile*. Charleston, SC: Arcadia Publishing, 2014.

———. *Kramer Williamson, Sprint Car Legend*. Jefferson, NC: McFarland & Company, 2017.

Newspapers and Periodicals

2011 Delaware International Speedway State Championship Program

2018 Camp Barnes Benefit Stock Car Race Program

Denton (MD) Journal, January 17, 1958

News Journal (DE), June 16, 1992

Internet References

ARRA. Documenting Racing History. sites.google.com/site/arradocumentingracinghistory.

Culver Auto Racing Museum. culverautoracingmuseum.com.

Delaware Racing. delawareracing.com.

Eastern Museum of Motor Racing. emmr.org.

Georgetown Speedway. thegeorgetownspeedway.com.

INDEX

P

R

S

T

U

V

W

ABOUT THE AUTHOR

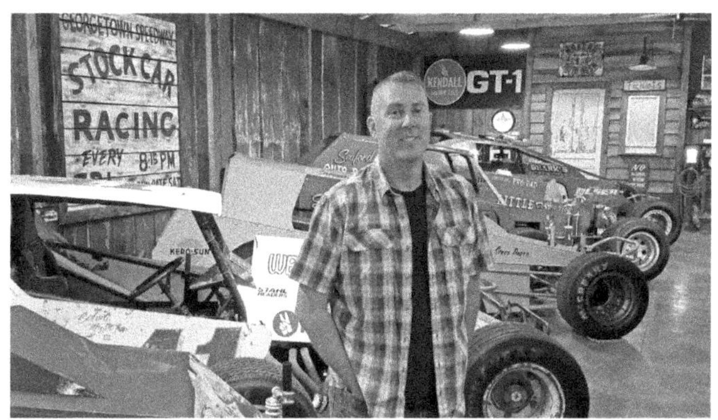

Chad Culver is a native of Laurel, Delaware, and is an author, racing historian, collector and director of the Culver Auto Racing Museum. Culver's other books on auto racing include *Delaware Auto Racing*, *Dover International Speedway: The Monster Mile* and *Kramer Williamson, Sprint Car Legend*. A lifelong fan of all things racing, Culver grew up in the shadow of Delaware International and Georgetown Speedways. With a passion for preserving history and collecting, Culver hopes to help document and preserve Delaware's racing history. When not working on his next book, he is busy working on his next restoration project for the museum. The Culver Auto Racing Museum houses an extensive collection of race cars and memorabilia from racing's past. Currently, he resides in North Carolina with his wife and daughter and returns home to Delaware often to attend every race he can.

www.ingramcontent.com/pod-product-compliance
Lightning Source LLC
LaVergne TN
LVHW052337100826
845147LV00020B/1094

9781467138291